A Pan and a Tin

by Cara Torrance

OXFORD
UNIVERSITY PRESS

a tin

Dad tips it in the tin.

a pan

Pat it in the pan.

a tin

Sit it in the tin.

Pat it and tap it.

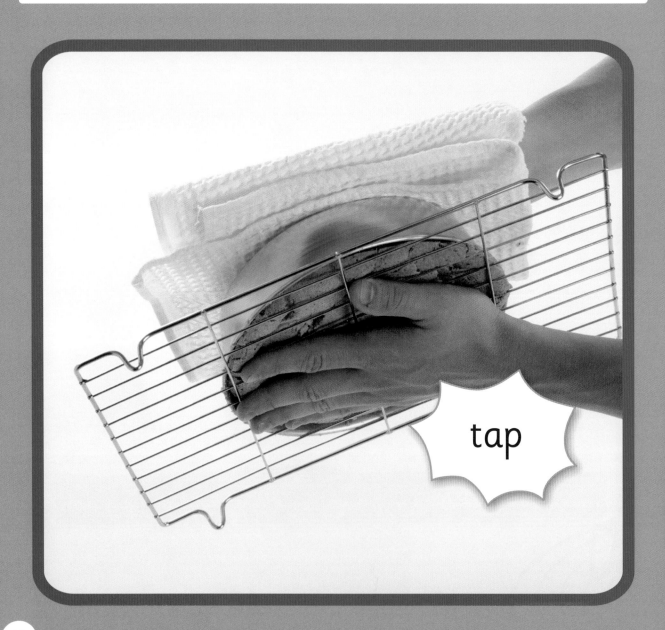

tap

a mat

Sam dips it in the pan.

I dip it in. I sip it.

A pan and a tin.

CAMPFIRE STORIES

CAPE COD

TALES & TRAVEL
COMPANION

edited by
ILYSSA KYU & DAVE KYU

MOUNTAINEERS
BOOKS

For our little barnacle and seal, Lula and Isla.
We'll always be your rock.

MOUNTAINEERS BOOKS is dedicated to the exploration, preservation, and enjoyment of outdoor and wilderness areas.

1001 SW Klickitat Way, Suite 201, Seattle, WA 98134
800-553-4453, www.mountaineersbooks.org

Printed in China

28 27 26 25   1 2 3 4 5

Design and layout: Melissa McFeeters

Library of Congress Cataloging-in-Publication data is on file for this title at https://lccn.loc.gov/2024947200

Mountaineers Books titles may be purchased for corporate, educational, or other promotional sales, and our authors are available for a wide range of events. For information on special discounts or booking an author, contact our customer service at 800-553-4453 or mbooks@mountaineersbooks.org.

Printed on FSC®-certified materials

ISBN (paperback): 978-1-68051-750-7
ISBN (ebook): 978-1-68051-751-4

An independent nonprofit publisher since 1960

Contents

CAPE COD STORIES

EXPLORE CAPE COD

Shaped by Wind and Waves

CAPE COD'S BEAUTY IS SUBTLE, void of the singular iconic peak or landmark by which we remember many of our beloved national parks. Most known as a summer retreat flanked by hundreds of miles of shoreline—40 miles of it protected within the Cape Cod National Seashore—Cape Cod conjures images of endless beach umbrellas, scantily clothed bodies soaking in the summer sun, and surfers buzzing around the crests of waves.

Each of its four regions—Upper Cape, Mid Cape, Lower Cape, and Outer Cape—has its own distinct personality and community. There are countless ways to spend your days outdoors on Cape Cod, like swimming at any point along the 500 miles of beaches, paddling or bird-watching on the nine hundred glacier-carved freshwater ponds and tidal salt marshes, pedaling across the whole Cape on the 25-mile Cape Cod Rail Trail, or fishing its abundant waters by boat or by land.

The fish that gave the Cape its name, once so plentiful they could be caught by scooping a basket through the water, have declined in population due to overfishing, but frequent visits by seals, sharks, and other marine mammals show that fish are still bountiful here.

Today, fishermen catch striped bass, bluefish, tautog, flounder, mackerel, scup, sea bass, lobster, oysters, and clams.

At one time, Portuguese fishermen and their families arrived in droves for the promise of jobs in the fishing and whaling industries, and they formed tight-knit communities and villages. Today their influence is still present in the region's culinary scene, where you might find dishes featuring linguiça, Portuguese sausage. But long before it was home to fishermen, sea captains, and lobstermen, and before it became muse and place of belonging for artists and LGBTQ+ communities, Cape Cod was the ancestral homeland of the Wampanoag ("People of the First Light"), whose territory stretched from present day eastern Rhode Island to Massachusetts. The Wampanoag were skilled fishermen, hunters, and farmers, and they lived in harmony with a land rich in fish, shellfish, and game, and which offered arable ground between forests. To maximize their use of this ground for crops, the Wampanoag used dead fish (Namâhsak) as fertilizer, placing them in the soil to add minerals before planting seeds. They planted corn (*Weeâchumuneash*), beans (*Tutupôhqâmash*), and squash (*Mônashk8tashqash*) together. This grouping is called the Three Sisters by various Indigenous peoples, as each plant supports the others' growth, and together they provide vital nutrients for a human diet.

After thriving on this land for thousands of years, the tribe experienced a catastrophe they came to call "the Great Dying." European traders brought illness that quickly spread among Native people, becoming a full-blown pandemic and killed nearly the entire Wampanoag population between approximately 1616 and 1619. Years before, European explorers had kidnapped Wampanoag sons, husbands, and fathers to sell as slaves across the world; if or when they returned to the Cape where they were born, they found their communities a graveyard, their friends and family succumbed to disease.

Today, the Mashpee Wampanoag Tribe—only federally recognized since 2007—has approximately 3200 enrolled citizens. A four-decades-long fight for tribal land resulted in the federal government declaring in 2015 just 300 acres of land in Mashpee and Taunton as tribal reservation. The other federally recognized present-day Wampanoag tribe, the Wampanoag Tribe of Gay Head (Aquinnah), lives on Martha's Vineyard (Noepe) and has more than 1300 enrolled citizens. Having dwelled there for ten thousand years, the Aquinnah Wampanoag now serve as caretakers of 477 acres of ancestral lands on the island set aside for their use and benefit. The Nauset Wampanoag, whose territory consisted largely of land on the Outer Cape, no longer exist as a separate tribe, but their bloodline and affiliation continue through the Mashpee Wampanoag Tribe.

While many people associate the Pilgrims with their landing at Plymouth, Massachusetts, they actually first landed on Cape Cod. There they buoyed their ships, took out smaller boats to explore Wampanoag territories, and wrote the Mayflower Compact. With their settlement came towns and industries centered around this region's rich resources, including timber, cranberries, fish, whales, and salt.

Pilgrims who arrived in 1620 saw the Great Dying as a sign from God that they were meant to colonize this land. In contrast to the Wampanoag people's balanced and wise use of the bounty from land and sea, the settlers' exploitation of resources drove significant changes to both. Oak and pine forests became heathlands after removal of the timber, and the oil rendered from the blubber of sperm whales brought in by Provincetown's whaling fleet illuminated and lubricated America's industrial growth in the early 1800s.

The commercial whaling industry first relied on "drift whales" stranded on Cape Cod beaches, but the harvest was unreliable, and when whaling became regulated by laws that forced communal profit sharing, New Englanders turned to the open sea for systematic hunting. The whaling industry only dwindled when the whale population declined and oil alternatives like petroleum emerged.

Seals, another native frequenting Cape Cod waters, were deemed a threat to fishing livelihoods and a nuisance to be dealt with. A bounty was put on gray seals, leading to the death of more than a hundred thousand at the hands of hunters between the 1890s and 1960s. Seal noses were exchanged for payment until the Marine Mammal Protection Act of 1972 outlawed their killing.

As the seal population recovers along Cape Cod, the region is seeing the return of its predator, the Atlantic white shark (also known as the great white shark), made infamous by films like Steven Spielberg's *Jaws* and Discovery Channel's *Shark Week*. Today, the boom in white shark activity triggers anxiety for beachgoers and builds tension among communities on Cape Cod. Native or not, the white sharks' prolific return makes them more menacing than welcome for families who've visited the Cape for generations. Some believe their carefree days of swimming and surfing Cape Cod's waters are over, a human-made issue caused by an overreach of the Marine Mammal Protection Act. To others this is a conservation success story, and sharks have simply found their way home thanks to a now thriving and balanced ecosystem.

Today, Cape Cod's population expands and contracts with the seasons. The Cape serves as a summer destination for millions of visitors each year, which locals consider a blessing and a curse as the influx of tourists helps power the economy and provide jobs, but puts a strain on the region's already limited resources, including solitude. The quieter, non-summer months are when locals and knowing travelers reap the rewards of this brilliantly abundant place. Once-packed beaches are dotted only by gray seals, migrating birds, and whatever the waves wash up along miles of shoreline.

This is among the most dynamic landscapes in the world, a glacial deposit with its long, muscled arm stretching out into the Atlantic, embracing Cape Cod Bay with an extended palm that over time, scientists say, will turn into a fist. The dunes that form cliffs and stunning lookout points over the great blue are continuously reshaping and shifting. Change is the natural constant here, something the community, culture, and people who inhabit this place have accepted and adapted to. Houses, lighthouses, and life-saving stations are constantly being picked up, floated down, and moved farther inland in response to the wind and water that continue to erode Cape Cod's shorelines.

When sunset and low tide align, you can view some of the most stunning displays of nature along the north coast of Cape Cod Bay, where miles of sand flats reflect the brilliant brushstrokes of the sky above. Tucked away in the nooks and crannies of the Cape are intertidal zones—areas that are regularly inundated by the tide and abundant with life. These breathtaking saltwater marshes, estuaries, and ponds serve as safe habitat for fishes and invertebrates, offering shelter and places to breed and forage. Grasses, sand, water, and seafoam dance in the wind. Stay a while and bear witness to how the tides and sunlight reveal new details before you.

The protected coastlines within the Cape Cod National Seashore invite you to hike, traversing through loose sand and over dunes to lighthouses and lookouts you can access only by foot or boat. Here, hiking is not about making good time or climbing the highest peaks. The landscape doesn't ask you to slow down, it compels you to. As Thoreau put it, "We made no haste, since we wished to see the ocean at our leisure; and indeed that soft sand was no place in which to be in a hurry, for one mile there was as good as two elsewhere."

Whether or not you're seeking perspective and introspection, this is a landscape that promises to shape you. For some it may define you. Perhaps that's how Provincetown, the outermost point of the cape, has come to be a queer capital of America. With its hypnotic shorelines of dunes and waves, Cape Cod has a storied history as a muse to many artists. In his introduction to later editions of Henry Beston's classic *The Outermost House*, nature writer and longtime Cape Cod resident Robert Finch writes, "This stretch of shoreline has been a remarkably fertile landfall for American nature writing." Writers, poets, and playwrights who are part of Cape Cod's literary tradition include Henry David Thoreau, Edna St. Vincent Millay, John Hay, Eugene O'Neill, Kurt Vonnegut, Stanley Kunitz, Mark Doty, and Mary Oliver.

Today, the legacy of artistic achievement lives on across the Cape but especially in Provincetown, where you'll find many art galleries, shops, and cultural centers—nearly all adorned with pride flags—and dune shacks offering artist residencies along the Outer Beach.

I (Ilyssa) did the travel and research for this book, while both Dave and I selected and edited pieces for the collection together—a very practical division of labor with two kids in school and Dave's full-time job. That's how I found myself in town during Women's

Week Provincetown, a celebration of LGBTQ+ women that brings in thousands of visitors each fall.

It's times like these when Provincetown feels like a place trapped in time. Traveling here during the off-season gave me a chance to recognize and feel the romance and energy of being in a culturally important place. Provincetown's narrow physical footprint made it almost impossible *not* to rub shoulders with local celebrities, comedians, drag queens, performers, and writers at the local bar once the summer crowds left. I felt starstruck by proxy when one of our contributors, Elizabeth Bradfield, shared that she used to be neighbors with *the* Mary Oliver—the iconic nature poet featured in this collection. Oliver moved to Provincetown in the 1960s to be with her longtime partner, Molly Malone Cook, and she wrote much of her prominent work in the fifty years she spent on Cape Cod. Despite being a huge fan of her writing and a poet herself, Liz felt Mary deserved her privacy and made sure to only talk to me about the weather or what they observed on hikes.

While there, I happened to catch Judy Gold at the landmark Post Office Cafe and Cabaret. A nationally renowned comedian with an HBO special and appearances on shows like *The Late Show with Stephen Colbert* and *The Tonight Show*, Judy is also a P-town local who's no stranger to performing multinight sets to try out new material.

During her set, Judy acknowledged her crowd—the LGBTQ+ women, trans, and nonbinary attendees—and took a moment to reflect on how unique and special Provincetown is. When people arrive, she explained, you know who is who from the direction of cars off Route 6. If they hang a right, with their trucks and American flags and fishing gear, you know they're there for the National Seashore. But if they hang a left, toward Provincetown, they're most certainly queer and about to have an experience they've been looking forward to the entire year, or perhaps their entire *life*. She described how coming to Provincetown, for many, was the first time they got to hold their partner's hand in public without the fear of being outed or judged. It's where love is love, and you're free to be yourself with whomever you love or just want to kiss for the night. Back in the day, sharing that you were going to Provincetown, she said, was the equivalent of *coming out*, so when asked where you were vacationing, you either lied or coolly said "Cape Cod," hoping people wouldn't ask you what *part* of the Cape. If they did, you had your answer ready with another town in the Upper, Mid, or Lower Cape—but *never* the Outer Cape.

While I generally pay little mind to my fashion choices, I was particularly proud that night of my bold nautical-striped top and bright autumnal pants. I was matching the season *and* the destination. If there is a quintessential Cape Cod vibe, I was convinced this was it and I was *feeling it*. As an introvert, I generally try to blend in, so naturally Judy found me during her crowd work portion of the evening. After she jokingly asked, "Is *anyone* here straight?" I raised my hand halfway, regretting it within a span of two seconds and shaking it in a teetering fashion to imply "straight-*ish*." In response, Judy quipped, "REALLY?! *You're* straight?! Well, a *lesbian* dressed you tonight, that's for sure!" . . . and she wasn't totally wrong.

Dave and I are happily married, with nineteen years and two kids between us, *and* I had recently come out as queer. For nearly all my life, I never really understood or accepted that I was queer, and I certainly didn't have the track record to claim it. As it became clearer as I got older, I was apprehensive to own or share that part of my identity out loud, to my loved ones or even to *myself*, having been married to a man for nearly two decades. I didn't know you were *allowed* to be queer and also in a happy hetero-passing marriage—or that both things could be true—so I learned to ignore it.

It wasn't until we were working on *Campfire Stories: Volume II*, seeking stories from marginalized writers for our collections, that my own sense of identity started to emerge. I began to reflect on how I had grown, changed, and learned a lot about myself since I was a sixteen-year-old grocery store bagger standing at the end of Dave's checkout line. While we were promoting our book on a month-long tour in the Pacific Northwest and Montana, I heard myself talking about the LGBTQ+ community as if I *wasn't* a part of it, and it started to feel dishonest . . . most acutely to *myself.* So I came out to Dave, and it has been one of the best gifts to myself and for our marriage. Before my trip to Cape Cod, we were the most communicative and honest we've ever been, and I was the happiest and most whole I've ever felt in my own body. The timing of this research trip felt like kismet in some ways.

Between interviews, museum visits, and hours scouring the shelves of libraries and bookstores, I spent time among the quiet marshes, dark and lily-dappled ponds, towering dunes, and relentless waves of the Atlantic—a luxury of time and space unfamiliar to me in the six years since becoming a parent. Following a hike around Blackwater Pond, a spot favored by Mary Oliver and inspiration for one of her most beloved poems, "In Blackwater Woods," I had an experience I can only describe as feeling like Oliver's spirit came and carried me to the ocean—lured by whale spouts off in the distance—and plopped me down in front of the waves and curious seals to write . . . a *poem.*

Unlike those who set out to follow in Thoreau's footsteps, hoping his path and written observations might help them find their own, I did not intended to write anything of my own, and certainly not a poem. The objective of this trip was to create a collection of stories written by *other people*. Without pen or paper, I stood before the ocean and words began pouring out of me. My thumbs fumbled to keep up with typing on my phone, as each word, each line flowed out with every pull of the waves—and for the first time in my adult life, I wrote a poem. And not just a poem, but a *queer* poem.

I had no business writing a poem about a place I had only just come to know, and yet it was one of the most transformative moments of my life. It seemed as though I, much like generations of writers before, had fallen under the spell of Cape Cod's ever-shifting and evolving shorelines. Despite having already come out, I only truly came to understand and accept myself in the moments among the dunes and pitch pine. With the landscape as my guide, I felt an immense sense of belonging—a quiet and knowing acceptance, the dunes teaching me how we all change shape over time.

The short stories, personal essays, and poems in this collection are just a few from the rich legacy of writers on Cape Cod, past and present. They're meant to be read around a "fire"—whether to yourself from the comfort of your couch or aloud to the people sharing the ember campfire glow with you. They are not stories for those seeking just to be entertained, but instead are for those curious about how this special region came to be and why it continues to mean so much to us. They are intended to communicate the essential character of the Cape: its diverse history, cultures, and people, and the experiences of those who have collectively built, shared, and enjoyed this place.

To identify themes and stories for this collection, we interviewed countless individuals who live and work here. We spent days inside libraries and bookstores along the Cape, and visited the region's rich natural and cultural landmarks—its dunes, marshes, and shorelines. We sought recommendations and insights from locals and combined them with our own experiences to create a guide that included practical tips for where to go, what to do, and where to camp, as well as ideas for how to visit in ways that respect and support the communities. Whether you've visited a hundred times or only through the pages of this book, we hope this collection deepens your connection to the Cape, allowing the region's landscape to show some of the ways that we all change shape, shift, and evolve over time.

Storytelling Tips

Storytelling has always been a fundamental part of being human. Beyond entertainment, stories have allowed us to share knowledge, traditions, and ideas, and to feel a sense of connection with people and places beyond our own experiences for thousands of years

Through all its forms, we have witnessed how stories can create deeper emotional connections between people and the natural world. This is especially true across generations and communities who have been disconnected from the outdoors, yet who are increasingly responsible for protecting it.

We believe that stories are best when they're shared with others, so we encourage you to share any stories or sections you love with friends or family, continuing in the tradition of oral storytelling, by sharing them aloud.

Should you find yourself gathered with others around a campfire, here are some tips for sharing a story:

Be prepared. A campfire can provide a warm, flickering light that sets the perfect mood, but it may not be adequate for reading a book, so bring a lantern, flashlight, headlamp, or book light. A glass of water can rescue you from a fit of coughing or a dry mouth, so keep it handy. In a camp setting with crickets and a crackling fire, you may be competing to be heard—sit or stand up straight, breathe from your diaphragm, and project your voice.

Choose the right story. Select a story that matches your audience's interests, age, attention span, and the moment. Pay attention to length; if it's too long, consider summarizing and read aloud only a particularly interesting or engaging poem or passage.

Introduce the story. Explain why you want to read this story, what it's about, and who wrote it—keeping it short and sweet. (Feel free to use our insider knowledge from the "About This Story" sections to get your audience excited.) End with a thought about what you took away from it and a question to engage your listeners.

Bring the story alive. Every story, especially poetry, has its own rhythm. When you read aloud, read it slightly faster than you would naturally speak but without rushing. Keep your listeners' attention by breaking up the rhythm with a long pause or a different cadence. (But don't overuse this trick or overperform!) Be authentic, enunciate clearly, and let your natural reactions enhance the story without disrupting the flow.

Most of all, have fun! Whether reading this book around a campfire, in your living room, at a park, or tucked cozily in bed, we hope you will find something that makes the natural world come alive.

The commonplace is defeated here,
by I know not what strangeness.
Once across the dunes we live
in an exquisite unreality.

✦

HAZEL HAWTHORNE,
SALT HOUSE (1934)

CAPE COD

STORIES

Wilderness

MICHAEL CUNNINGHAM

Excerpts from *Land's End:*
A Walk in Provincetown

Although the desks in the schools are no longer half buried in sand, and sand-drifts no longer pile up against the walls of houses, Provincetown is still thoroughly infiltrated by its skittish, sandy wilderness. Auto body shops stand in the shadows of dunes; the waterfront houses are built directly on sand and have shells and beach grass where their inland sisters would have lawns. There is no place where you can't hear the foghorn. The wilderness offers escape from the noise and commerce; town offers at least partial sanctuary from the abiding patience out there, that which sifts through your windows at night and will be there long after you are gone.

In a sense Provincetown *is* a beach. If you stand on the shore watching the tide recede, you are merely that much closer to the water and that much more available to weather than you would be in the middle of town. All along the bay side, the entire length of town, the beach slopes gently, bearded with kelp and dry sea grass. Because Provincetown stands low on the continental shelf, it is profoundly affected by tides, which can exceed a twelve-foot drop at the syzygy of sun, moon, and earth. Interludes of beach that are more than a hundred yards wide at low tide vanish entirely when the tide is high. The water of the bay is utterly calm in most weathers and warmer than that of the ocean beaches, but this being the North Atlantic, no water anywhere is ever what you could rightfully call warm, not even in August. Except in extreme weather the bay beach is entirely domesticated, the backyard of the town, never empty but never crowded, either; there is no surf there, and the water that laps docilely up against the shore is always full of boats. The bay beach is especially good for dogs and small children, whose only other access to large, untrammeled space is the playing field of the high school on the hill. The bay beach is also good for strolling along in solitude, which is most satisfying, to me, on clear winter days, when the air is almost painfully sharp and scraps of snow linger on the sand. The beach is strewn with shells, but they are New England shells, almost exclusively bivalves, running from gray to brown to lighter brown with minor hints of mauve or deep, dusty purple. This is not a marine landscape prone to pinks or pale blues. The beach does yield the occasional treasure, an old clay pipe or a whole glass bottle that the ocean has turned opalescent. Paul Bowen, a sculptor who combs the beaches incessantly, has even found a few porcelain dolls' heads, arms, and legs over the years, and I always walk along that section hoping to see a tiny white face, half buried in sand, offering prim scarlet lips and one empty blue eye from among the stones and shards.

Long Point

The remotest end of the sandy spiral on which Provincetown stands—the very tip of the Cape's languidly unfurling hook—is

called Long Point, a narrow scrap of dunes and grass. It is tenta-
tively part of the mainland, but centuries ago the ocean dissolved
most of the scrawny neck of sand that connected it. There is now
a jetty that attaches Long Point to the far West End, built in 1911.
In the 1700s, though, when Long Point was essentially an island, a
community started up there, and eventually it grew to about two
hundred people, most of whom operated salt works, where sea
water was evaporated for salt. Everything these citizens needed,
everything the Atlantic didn't provide, was brought over by boat
from Provincetown proper.

During the War of 1812 the British occupied Provincetown
and cut off supplies to the people on Long Point. When the Civil
War broke out, the people of Provincetown, fearing that the Con-
federate Army would invade and set up a similar blockade, built
two fortresses of sand on Long Point, with a cannon in each. The
Confederates never came anywhere near Provincetown, however,
and as volunteers stood guard day after day and night after night
over an uncontested stretch of salt water, the fortresses came to
be known as Fort Useless and Fort Ridiculous.

Before the Civil War, toward the middle of the 1800s, the citizens
of Long Point began to feel that they'd made a mistake in settling
there at all. Their houses were almost flirtatiously available to
gales and hurricanes, their salt wasn't selling as it once had, and
the notion that every egg, darning needle, or pair of socks had
to be ordered and delivered by boat had lost its charm. So they
had their houses, forty-eight of them, jacked up, loaded onto
barges, and floated over to the mainland. Most of the old houses
in Provincetown, being built on sand, had no foundations at all
and could be moved from one place to another without much
more difficulty than what would be involved in transporting a

drydocked boat across land. On the mainland houses perched at the tops of dunes were known sometimes to work their way down slowly, over the years, until they rested at the feet of the dunes they had once crested.

The houses that were floated over from Long Point still stand, mostly in the West End of Provincetown, though there are a few in the East End as well. Each of them bears a blue plaque, with a picture of a house on a barge floating calmly over white squiggles of unprotesting waves.

At the tide's lowest point you can walk to Long Point from the West End, over the expanse of wet sand. You can walk there, regardless of the tides, across the jetty that starts at the far west end of Commercial Street. The jetty is a thirty-foot-wide ribbon of rough granite blocks that extends almost to its own vanishing point when you stand on the mainland looking out to Long Point. You may want to walk all the way to the point, or you may just want to go partway out and sit on the rocks for a while. In summer, an hour or so before high tide, when the water is moving in, you can slide in from the rocks and let yourself be carried along by the tide, almost all the way back to shore.

If you do walk to Long Point, you will find yourself on a spit of sand about three hundred yards wide, with bay beach on one side, ocean beach on the other, and a swatch of dune grass running down the middle. It sports, like an austere ornament, a lighthouse and a long-empty shed once used to store oil for the light. You will be almost alone there, though the water around you will be thoroughly populated by boats. It is a favorite nesting ground for terns and gulls. When I went out there years ago with Christy, the man with whom I lived then, he strode into the dune grass and stirred up the birds. If I tell you that he stood exultantly among hundreds of shrieking white birds that circled and swooped furiously around him, looking just like a figure out of Dante, grinning majestically, while I stood by and worried about what it was doing to the birds, you may know everything you need to know about why we were together and why we had to part.

The Salt Marsh

Just beyond the jetty, past the hairpin curve Commercial Street makes as it turns back on itself and changes its name to Bradford Street, is the salt marsh. The long road that starts at the landward end of Cape Cod ends here, at this wild lawn of sea grass. The marsh reliably tells the time, the state of the weather, and the season: emerald in spring and summer, gold in fall, various browns in winter. Wind when it blows raises flashes and swells of paler color among the grasses and reeds, so you can stand at the edge of the marsh and see just how strongly the wind is blowing, and in what direction. Because the marsh is always at least partly flooded, reflected sky lights the grass from below. On sunny days it can seem unnaturally bright, and on cloudy days it looks even brighter.

It is puddled during low tides, inundated when the tide is high. It terminates in a range of dunes, beyond which is the ocean, though you can't see it from where you now stand. You may see a heron or two, wading among the tidal pools. You will assuredly see the little white thumb of Wood End lighthouse, far away. (It is not the one on Long Point.) I've never gone there and don't intend to. I know—or rather, I can imagine—that up close it's merely an old plaster tower, its paint cracked and peeling, spattered all over its concrete base with seagull shit. I prefer that it remain a distant object, its romance undiluted, an image out of Virginia Woolf. I believe every city and town should contain at least one remote

spot, preferably a beautiful and mysterious one, that you see but
never visit. . . .

The Dunes

Behind the beach at Herring Cove, behind all of Provincetown, is
the Cape Cod National Seashore, established during the Kennedy
administration as a recreation area and nature preserve. Whatever
our feelings about John F. Kennedy as president, we can be grateful
to him for that. The town cannot expand past a certain point; no
one can build a resort hotel in the dunes or on the ocean beaches.
The dunes are an intact ecosystem, as particular unto themselves
as Zion in Utah or the Florida Everglades, though unlike Zion or
the Everglades they were formed, in part, by man. Early settlers
felled the trees for fuel and lumber, and replanted the landscape
with pitch pine and scrub oak. With the big trees gone, a sand-sea
began working its methodical way in from the beaches, and what
you are seeing in this sedate landscape is actually an ongoing
process of erosion.

   The best way to go through the dunes is on a bicycle, which
you can rent from one of four places in town. A single snake of
trail, not conspicuously marked, starts from the far end of the
parking lot at Herring Cove and winds through the dunes. The
dunescape is simultaneously verdant and lunar. It is dotted with
brush and scrubby, stunted pine. It has a smell: pine and salt, with
an undercurrent of something I can only describe as dusty and
green. In patches the landscape is almost pure sand, pristine as
sugar. The sandy areas seem primeval in their silence and shadows,
though they are, of course, not ancient at all—they weren't like
this a hundred years ago; a century from now they will be visibly
different. Still, I often feel when I'm out there that I'm palpably on

the surface of a planet, with a thin illusion of blue overhead and the universe beyond. It is especially wonderful to ride through the dunes at night, when the moon is full.

In these same dunes but miles up Cape, too far for biking, is the place where Guglielmo Marconi first tested the telegraph—where a human being was able, for the first time, to send and receive wireless messages across the Atlantic. The building in which he conducted his experiment has since fallen into the ocean, but a weathered gazebo bearing a plaque stands today to commemorate the spot where, over a hundred years ago, Marconi sat day after day and night after night, convinced that he could communicate not only with those living on other continents but with the dead as well. He thought sound waves did not vanish over time; he believed he could find a way to hear the cries of men on ships sunk long ago, the voices of children whose own children were ancient by then, the musket reports of Columbus's men as they showed the Tecumwah tribe what terrible new gods had arrived on their shores. . . .

The Beech Forest

If you go straight on the dune trail and skip Race Point, you will eventually reach the beech forest. There is a clear point of demarcation between the sand and the woods it has partially engulfed. First you will see what appear to be outcroppings of bare twigs protruding from the sand—these are the tops of dead trees. Several yards farther on you will see dead trees mired to their lower branches in sand, and then trees that are covered only halfway up their trunks, still alive but beginning to die. Then you will be among the living trees. The sand-glacier in the beech forest has been more or less halted by conservationists, but the dunes north of the forest remain in motion. On old maps you can locate buried forests, and walk across pristine dunes with deceased forests inside them.

The beech forest in summer is shady and slightly dank; it is full of a greened, deepened light. The smell changes from dusty pine to a fermented odor of pine tar, decomposing leaves, and an indefinable, organic rankness that resembles, at its most potent, the smell of a wet dog. You will pass a shallow pond that freezes over in winter and that wears, in summer, a skin of pale green lily pads with trumpet-shaped flowers—yellow at the edges of the pond, white in the slightly deeper water toward the middle. You can stay on the narrow asphalt bike trail, or you can leave your bike and wander into the woods along any of the sandy paths that meander off among the trees. If you do that, you'll quickly find yourself walking among tupelo and inkberry, white oaks and red maples, as well as the eponymous beech trees, all of which form surprisingly orderly hallways and small, room-like clearings, with lush carpets of fallen leaves and canopies of branches thick enough to shelter you in a rainstorm. It would not be entirely surprising to find chairs and lamps out there, and a table set for tea. People sometimes get married in these clearings, and local children go there for all the childish purposes that require concealment. The trunks of the trees are covered with carvings: initials and obscenities; various assertions that so-and-so was here, in 1990 or 1975 or 1969; declarations of eternal love to vanished objects named Jim, Carol, Drew, Calla, Tom, Ken, and Lindy, among others. The old ones, from the fifties and sixties, have all but faded into the bark—they look like name-shaped scars manifested by the trees themselves. The newer ones are various shades of gray, depending on their age. Only the very recent names are raw and white, though they too, of course, will fade.

Snail Road

The last wild place on land I want to tell you about is the dune at the end of Snail Road. Snail Road is actually a dirt path, though wide enough to accommodate a car, and you can in fact park your car there if you need to. It is on the East End of town, on the far side of the highway. The path is arcaded by the branches of trees. At its far end stands the dune known as Mt. Ararat, a single, titanic rise of sand, utterly barren. It could be a dune in the Sahara.

This is another of those strangely potent places. Everyone I know who has spent any time on the dune agrees that there's, well, *something* there, though outwardly it is neither more nor less than an enormous arc of sand cutting across the sky. Climb to the top of it. On one side you'll see the treetops and rooftops of town; on the other you'll look across a span of lesser dunes to the Atlantic. To the east, in the direction of Truro, is Pilgrim Lake, though you can't quite see it from atop Mt. Ararat. Pilgrim Lake was once East Harbor but is now, essentially, an enormous puddle. About 150 years ago, the town fathers realized that windblown sand was accumulating in East Harbor in such quantities that it threatened not only to render the harbor too shallow for boats but might extend out along the coast and spoil all of Provincetown's harbor. So they diked off East Harbor and laid railroad tracks on the new embankment that separated it from the open water. The only road into Provincetown still runs along that embankment, parallel to the long-vanished train tracks.

Being stilled and sourceless, Pilgrim Lake feels vaguely sinister. It is Provincetown's Dead Sea. Although it is every bit as bright in sunlight as the ocean from which it has been separated, it shimmers differently. It is steelier, more opaque. From the dune at the end of Snail Road, you are surrounded by the Atlantic in three different aspects: the ocean proper, the bay, and the brackish lake.

The lunar stillness that pervades out there is difficult to describe. It involves a repose that is pleasurable without being exactly comforting. You feel as if you are in the eye of something. You are aware—I am aware, anyway—of the world as a place that doesn't know or care that it's beautiful, that produces beauty incidentally while pursuing its true imperatives to simply exist and change; a world that is, more than anything else, silent and unpopulated as it lives according to geological time. You feel, momentarily, what I imagine nomads might feel as they cross the desert. You are at home, and you are at the same time in a place too full of its own eternal business, too old and too young, to notice whether you live or die, you with your pots and pans and rugs and bells.

About This Story

Michael Cunningham's 2012 book *Land's End: A Walk in Province-town* is the perfect companion on a trip to Cape Cod. It's a staple of bookstores along the Cape and Islands Bookstore Trail, and can even be spotted at souvenir shops in town. This book feels like a friend who has long lived, *really lived*, in between the dunes and tight streets of Provincetown. Cunningham lives in New York City but regularly spent time on Cape Cod before his Pulitzer Prize–winning book *The Hours* was adapted for a film in 2002, enabling him to purchase a hundred-year-old Provincetown home that was once an inn. He says in an interview, "I love Provincetown. I love it more unreservedly than I love any other place. I am totally aware of its drawbacks, peculiarities, and absurdities."

That comes through in his book, which excels at highlighting the quirks of P-town's people, culture, and community. We loved this chapter offering vignettes from the different landscapes of the town's neighboring wilderness. During breakfast in Provincetown, we pored over these pages as armchair hikers trekking right along on this guided tour of the dunes, forests, marshes, and beaches of Cape Cod. If you're interested in some of the less family-friendly sections of the chapter, which we've left out, we suggest you pick up this Cape Cod classic.

Rock

MARY PETIET

Rock sits the size of a Mini-Cooper
in my front yard
along the Old King's Highway,
and that's just the part you can see.

For all I know,
Rock goes deep into the earth
possibly emerging in China,
and right now a Chinese writer
is puzzling out a story about this immovable rock
occupying prime real estate
on her own front lawn.

23,000 years ago Cape Cod
was born of an ice sheet.

The receding ice
left the long arm of the Cape
jutting into the cold Atlantic
piled with rocks, lined with scars

pocked with kettle holes
brimming icy afterbirth.

We live atop a scene of ancient devastation.

The noise of all those tons
of moving rock and ice
must have been deafening,
but today I hear
the springtime chirp of tree frogs,
emerging from hibernation
deep within the loamy depths
of the kettle hole near Rock.

A pair of ducks return here annually
with ducklings in mind,
quiet hatching to counter
the land's ancient booming.

I sit on Rock warm in the spring sun
feeling the ages
feeling the energy flowing through Rock
as surely as it flows
through us all in mute connection.

Can Rock remember the primeval time
before man came to our narrow land,
time of saber tooth tigers
wandering the sand flats,
the time of unrecognizable beasts
dotting the surf?

Then the time of the first people,
wanderers from beyond
the Bering Strait probing south and east
for good game and fishing
and settling to establish a footpath past Rock.

Soft moccasined feet passed Rock,
until suddenly leather boots
traversed the beaten dirt
and the path widened into a road,
and horses and wagons
joined the traffic.

Booted people built my house
and still Rock sat too big to move,
ensconced between the house and the road
watching the people glean a hard-won life
from inhospitable soil.

Miles of stone walls were built
from smaller movable rocks,
each pulled painfully from
the earth by teams of oxen,
and still Rock watched
as farmers switched to sheep
for an easier living.

Pavement was laid
and phone poles raised
and street lights began greeting the dusk,
and Rock suddenly no longer knew

true dark,
and tried to remember
true black night.

Now Rock knows
summer traffic and winter plows,
the daily school bus and the paperboy.

Rock knows us.

Does Rock remember?

Sitting upon Rock in the spring warmth,

I remember.

About This Story

It was Henry David Thoreau's writing that introduced most Americans to Cape Cod, but historians agree that Thoreau's Cape Cod was radically different from the Cape we know today, or what it had once been. In the mid-1800s, the area was frequented by urban sportsmen who occupied the various hunting and fishing camps to catch wild game. Before that, though, the industries of shipbuilding and saltworks—huge wooden vats where saltwater was evaporated to harvest salt—extracted so much timber from the Cape's forests that Thoreau saw a barren landscape of "scrubby wood," even though the Pilgrims spoke of fine soil and varied woods when they arrived in the 1690s. The Wampanoag people had lived in balance with the abundant ocean, forest, and beach landscapes of yet another Cape

Cod. And twenty thousand years before they arrived, the shifting glaciers carved the foundation of this landscape.

All the features of the Cape have altered as human settlement, changing climate, and natural evolution shift the land underneath this dynamic place. Well, almost all, Mary Petiet imagines, as Rock bears witness to a world that transforms around it. Petiet's work as an author, poet, and publisher is deeply influenced by the natural environment of Cape Cod and its inspirational energy. Both her book *Moon Tide: Cape Cod Poems* and her novel *Wash Ashore: A Tale of Cape Cod* are infused with the nature and lore of Cape Cod. In 2020 she founded Sea Crow Press, an independent publisher dedicated to amplifying the voices of humans, animals, and the land.

The Year at High Tide

HENRY BESTON

Excerpt from *The Outermost House*

I

Had I room in this book, I should like to write a whole chapter on the sense of smell, for all my life long I have had of that sense an individual enjoyment. To my mind, we live too completely by the eye. I like a good smell—the smell of a freshly ploughed field on a warm morning after a night of April rain, the clovelike aroma of our wild Cape Cod pinks, the morning perfume of lilacs showery with dew, the good reek of hot salt grass and low tide blowing from these meadows late on summer afternoons....

One reason for my love of this great beach is that, living here, I dwell in a world that has a good natural smell, that is full of keen, vivid, and interesting savours and fragrances. I have them at their best, perhaps, when hot days are dulled with a warm rain. So well do I know them, indeed, that were I blindfolded and led about the summer beach, I think I could tell on what part of it I was at any moment standing. At the ocean's very edge the air is almost always cool—cold even—and delicately moist with surf spray and the endless dissolution of the innumerable bubbles of the foam slides; the wet sand slope beneath exhales a cool savour of mingling beach and sea, and the innermost breakers push ahead of them puffs of this fragrant air. It is a singular experience to walk this brim of ocean when the wind is blowing almost directly down the beach, but now veering a point toward the dunes, now a point toward the sea. For twenty feet a humid and tropical exhalation of hot, wet sand encircles one, and from this one steps, as through a door, into as many yards of mid-September. In a point of time, one goes from Central America to Maine.

Atop the broad eight-foot back of the summer bar, inland forty feet or so from the edge of low tide, other odours wait. Here have the tides strewn a moist tableland with lumpy tangles, wisps, and matted festoons of ocean vegetation—with common sea grass, with rockweed olive-green and rockweed olive-brown, with the crushed and wrinkled green leaves of sea lettuce, with edible, purple-red dulse and bleached sea moss, with slimy and gelatinous cords seven and eight feet long. In the hot noontide they lie, slowly, slowly withering—for their very substance is water—and sending an odour of ocean and vegetation into the burning air. I like this good natural savour. Sometimes a dead, surf-trapped fish, perhaps a dead skate curling up in the heat, adds to this odour of vegetation a faint fishy rankness, but the smell is not earth corruption, and the scavengers of the beach soon enough remove the cause.

Beyond the bar and the tidal runnel farther in, the flat region I call the upper beach runs back to the shadeless bastion of the dunes. In summer this beach is rarely covered by the tides. Here lies a hot and pleasant odour of sand. I find myself an angle of shade slanting off from a mass of wreckage still embedded in a dune, take up a handful of the dry, bright sand, sift it slowly through my fingers, and note how the heat brings out the fine, sharp, stony smell of it. There is weed here, too, well buried in the dry sand—flotsam of last month's high, full-moon tides. In the shadowless glare, the topmost fronds and heart-shaped air sacs have ripened to an odd iodine orange and a blackish iodine brown. Overwhelmed thus by sand and heat, the aroma of this foliage has dissolved; only a shower will summon it again from these crisping, strangely coloured leaves.

Cool breath of eastern ocean, the aroma of beach vegetation in the sun, the hot, pungent exhalation of fine sand—these mingled are the midsummer savour of the beach.

II

In my open, treeless world, the year is at flood tide. All day long and all night long, for four days and five days, the southwest wind blows across the Cape with the tireless constancy of a planetary river. The sun, descending the altar of the year, pauses ritually on the steps of the summer months, the disk of flame over-flowing. On hot days the beach is tremulous with rising, visible heat bent seaward by the wind; a blue haze hangs inland over the moors and the great marsh blotting out pictorial individualities and reducing the landscape to a mass. Dune days are sometimes hotter than village days, for the naked glare of sand reflects the heat; dune nights are always cooler. On its sun-trodden sand, between the marsh wind and the coolness of ocean, the Fo' castle has been as comfortable as a ship at sea.

The duneland air burns with the smell of sand, ocean, and sun. On the tops of the hills, the grass stands at its tallest and greenest, its new straw-green seed plumes rising through a dead crop of last year's withered spears. On some leaves there is already a tiny spot of orange wither at the very tip, and thin lines of wither descending on either edge. Grasses in the salt meadows are fruiting; there are brownish and greenish-yellow patches on the levels of summer green. On the dunes, the sand lies quiescent in a tangle of grass; in naked places, it lies as if it were held down by the sun. When there has been no rain for a week or more, and the slanting flame has been heavy on the beach, the sand in my path down Fo'castle dune becomes so dry, so loose and deep, that I trudge through it as through snow.

The winter sea was a mirror in a cold, half-lighted room, the summer sea is a mirror in a room burning with light. So abundant is the light and so huge the mirror that the whole of a summer day floats reflected on the glass. Colours gather there, sunrise and twilight, cloud shadows and cloud reflections, the pewter dullness of gathering rain, the blue, burning splendour of space swept free of every cloud. Light transfixes ocean, and some warmth steals in with the light, but the waves that glint in the sun are still a tingling cold. . . .

III

The most interesting adventure with birds I have had this summer I had with a flock of least terns, *Sterna antillarum.* It came to pass that early one morning in June, as I happened to be passing big dune, a covey of small terns unexpectedly sailed out at me and hovered about me, scolding and complaining. To my great delight, I saw that they were least terns or "tit gulls," rare creatures on our coast, and perhaps the prettiest and most graceful of summer's ocean birds. A miniature tern, the "leastie," scarce larger than a swallow, and you may know him by the lighter grey of his plumage, his bright lemon-yellow bill, and his delicate orange-yellow feet.

The birds were nesting at the foot of big dune, and I had disturbed their peace. In the splendour of morning they hung above me, now uttering a single alarmed cheep, now a series of staccato cries.

I walked over to the nests.

The nest of such a beach bird is a singular affair. It is but a depression, and sometimes scarcely that, in the open, shelterless beach. "Nest building on the open sand," says Mr. Forbush, "is but the work of a moment. The bird alights, crouches slightly, and works its little feet so rapidly that the motion seems a mere blur, while the sand flies out in every direction as the creature pivots about. The tern then settles lower and smooths the cavity by turning and working and moving its body from side to side."

I have mislaid the scrap of paper on which I jotted down the number of nests I found that morning, but I think I counted twenty to twenty-five. There were eggs in every nest, in some two, in others three, in one case and one only, four. To describe the coloration of the shells is difficult, for there was a deal of variation, but perhaps I can give some idea of their appearance by saying that they were beach-coloured with overtones of bluish green, and speckled with browns and violet-browns and lavenders. What interested me most, however, was not the eggs, but the manner in which the birds had decorated their nests with pebbles and bits of shell. Here and there along the beach, the "leasties" had picked up fat bits of sea shell about the size of a finger nail and with these bits they had lined the bowl or their nests, setting the flat pieces in flat, like parts of a mosaic.

For two weeks I watched these "leasties" and their nests, taking every precaution not to disturb or alarm the setting birds. Yet I had but to pass anywhere between them and the tide to put them up, and when I walked south with coast guardsmen, I heard single cries of alarm in the starry and enormous night. Toward the end of June, a sudden northeaster came.

It was a night storm. I built a little fire, wrote a letter or two, and listened to the howling wind and the bursts of rain. All night long, and it was a wakeful, noisy night, I had the "leasties" on my mind. I felt them out there on the wild shelterless beach, with the black gale screaming over them and the rain pouring down. Opening my door, I looked for a moment into the drenching blackness and heard a great roaring of the sea.

The tide and the gale had ebbed together when I rose at five the next morning, but there was still wind and a grey drizzle. At the foot of big dune I found desolation. The tide had swept the beach. Not a nest remained or a sign of a nest, and the birds had gone. Later that day, just south of big dune, I saw bits of bluish-green eggshell in a lump of fresh weed. Where the birds went to, I never knew. Probably to a better place to try again. . . .

I must now add a paragraph from my autumnal notes and tell of my last sight of the great summer throng of terns. It was an unforgettable experience. During August the birds thinned out, and as the month drew to a close, whole days passed without a sight or sign of their presence. By September 1st, I imagined that most of them had gone. Then came the unexpected. On Saturday, September 3d, friends came down the beach to see me, and at the close of their visit, as I opened the Fo' castle door, I found that the air above the dunes was snowy with young terns.

The day had been mild, and the late afternoon light was mild and rosy golden—the sun was an hour from his setting—and high in space and golden light the myriads of birds drifted and whirled like leaves. North and south we saw them for miles along the dunes.

For twenty minutes, perhaps, or half an hour, the swarming filled my sky, and during all that time I did not hear a single bird utter a single sound.

At the end of that period, withdrawing south and inland, the gathering melted away.

It was really a very curious thing. Apparently some impulse from heaven had suddenly seized upon the birds, entered into their feathered breasts, and led them into the air above the dunes. Whence came that spirit, whence its will, and how had it breathed its purpose into those thousand hearts? The whole performance reminded me very much of a swarming of bees. A migrational impulse, yes, and something more. The birds were flying high, higher than I had ever seen terns go, and as far as I could judge— or guess—the great majority of the fliers were young birds of the year. It was a rapture, a glory of the young. And this was the last of the terns. . . .

IV

The other day I saw a young swimmer in the surf. He was, I judged, about twenty-two years old and a little less than six feet tall, splendidly built, and as he stripped I saw that he must have been swimming since the season began, for he was sunburned and brown. Standing naked on the steep beach, his feet in the climbing seethe, he gathered himself for a swimmer's crouching spring, watched his opportunity, and suddenly leaped headfirst through a long arc of air into the wall of a towering and enormous wave. Again and again he repeated his jest, emerging each time beyond the breaker with a stare of salty eyes, a shake of the head, and a smile. It was all a beautiful thing to see: the surf thundering across the great natural world, the beautiful and compact body in its naked strength and symmetry, the astounding plunge across the air, arms extended ahead, legs and feet together, the emerging stroke of the flat hands, and the alternate rhythms of the sunburned and powerful shoulders.

Watching this picture of a fine human being free for the moment of everything save his own humanity and framed in a scene of nature, I could not help musing on the mystery of the human body and of how nothing can equal its rich and rhythmic beauty when it is beautiful or approach its forlorn and pathetic ugliness when beauty has not been mingled in or has withdrawn. Poor body, time and the long years were the first tailors to teach you the merciful use of clothes! Though some scold to-day because you are too much seen, to my mind, you are not seen fully enough or often enough when you are beautiful. All my life it has given me pleasure to see beautiful human beings. To see beautiful young men and women gives one a kind of reverence for humanity (alas, of how few experiences may this be said), and surely there are few moods of the spirit more worthy of our care than those in which we reverence, even for a moment, our tragic and bewildered kind.

About This Story

If Henry David Thoreau hadn't written *Cape Cod*, author and naturalist Henry Beston would certainly take his spot as the foundational writer of the region. Beston's *The Outermost House*, first published in 1928, is a literary work as essential to Cape Cod as Thoreau's *Walden* is to the woods of Massachusetts. Both writers capture their time in isolation with keen observations of their surroundings—for Beston, the expansiveness and fury of the sea, for Thoreau, the changing moods of a small pond in a woodland setting. At one point in creating this collection, Dave asked Ilyssa, "Do we *have* to include Henry Beston?" Ilyssa gawked at Dave as if he had suggested writing a guidebook to Paris without mentioning the Eiffel Tower.

Much like Thoreau's writing, Henry Beston's book has contributed to and inspired the literary canon that is Cape Cod—making it one of the most referenced pieces of literature from a region whose suggestive landscape has been written about over the centuries by "an extraordinary number of essayists, poets, and novelists." Robert Finch points this out in his introduction to later editions of *The Outermost House*, going on to say, "Few, if any, natural areas of comparable size on the continent have been written about so extensively and so well, perhaps in part because this meeting place of land and sea—of the gentle, human-scaled contours of the Cape's soft sands and the protean, formless wilderness of the open ocean— allows us to see what we need to see, providing us with the raw materials of personality and voice." We include Henry Beston not out of obligation but for his ability to make meaning of what one can witness—and smell—on the dunes at the edge of the sea.

The Wellfleet Whale

STANLEY KUNITZ

A few summers ago, on Cape Cod, a whale foundered on the beach, a sixty-three-foot finback whale. When the tide went out, I approached him. He was lying there, in monstrous desolation, making the most terrifying noises—rumbling—groaning. I put my hands on his flanks and I could feel the life inside him. And while I was standing there, suddenly he opened his eye. It was a big, red, cold eye, and it was staring directly at me. A shudder of recognition passed between us. Then the eye closed forever. I've been thinking about whales ever since.

—JOURNAL ENTRY

I

You have your language too,
　　　　an eerie medley of clicks
　　　　　　　　hoots and trills,
location-notes and love calls,
　　　　whistles and grunts. Occasionally,
　　　　　　　　it's like furniture being smashed,
or the creaking of a mossy door,
　　　　sounds that all melt into a liquid

song with endless variations,
as if to compensate
for the vast loneliness of the sea.
Sometimes a disembodied voice
breaks in, as if from distant reefs,
and it's as much as one can bear
to listen to its long mournful cry,
a sorrow without name, both more
and less than human. It drags
across the ear like a record
running down.

II

No wind. No waves. No clouds.
Only the whisper of the tide,
as it withdrew, stroking the shore,
a lazy drift of gulls overhead,
and tiny points of light
bubbling in the channel.
It was the tag-end of summer.
From the harbor's mouth
you coasted into sight,
flashing news of your advent,
the crescent of your dorsal fin
clipping the diamonded surface.
We cheered at the sign of your greatness
when the black barrel of your head
erupted, ramming the water,
and you flowered for us
in the jet of your spouting.

III

All afternoon you swam
    tirelessly round the bay,
        with such an easy motion,
the slightest downbeat of your tail,
    an almost imperceptible
        undulation of your flippers,
you seemed like something poured,
    not driven; you seemed
        to marry grace with power.
And when you bounded into air,
    slapping your flukes,
        we thrilled to look upon
pure energy incarnate
    as nobility of form.
        You seemed to ask of us
not sympathy, or love,
    or understanding,
        but awe and wonder.

That night we watched you
    swimming in the moon.
        Your back was molten silver.
We guessed your silent passage
    by the phosphorescence in your wake.
        At dawn we found you stranded on the rocks.

IV

There came a boy and a man
    and yet other men running, and two
        schoolgirls in yellow halters

and a housewife bedecked
       with curlers, and whole families in beach
             buggies with assorted yelping dogs.
The tide was almost out.
       We could walk around you,
             as you heaved deeper into the shoal,
crushed by your own weight,
       collapsing into yourself,
             your flippers and your flukes
quivering, your blowhole
       spasmodically bubbling, roaring.
             In the pit of your gaping mouth
you bared your fringework of baleen,
       a thicket of horned bristles.
             When the Curator of Mammals
arrived from Boston
       to take samples of your blood
             you were already oozing from below.
Somebody had carved his initials
       in your flank. Hunters of souvenirs
             had peeled off strips of your skin,
a membrane thin as paper.
       You were blistered and cracked by the sun.
             The gulls had been pecking at you.
The sound you made was a hoarse and fitful bleating.

What drew us to the magnet of your dying?
       You made a bond between us,
             the keepers of the nightfall watch,
who gathered in a ring around you,
       boozing in the bonfire light.

Toward dawn we shared with you
your hour of desolation,
        the huge lingering passion
                of your unearthly outcry,
as you swung your blind head
        toward us and laboriously opened
                a bloodshot, glistening eye,
in which we swam with terror and recognition.

V

Voyager, chief of the pelagic world,
        you brought with you the myth
                of another country, dimly remembered,
where flying reptiles
        lumbered over the steaming marshes
                and trumpeting thunder lizards
wallowed in the reeds.
        While empires rose and fell on land,
                your nation breasted the open main,
rocked in the consoling rhythm
        of the tides. Which ancestor first plunged
                head-down through zones of colored twilight
to scour the bottom of the dark?
        You ranged the North Atlantic track
                from Port-of-Spain to Baffin Bay,
edging between the ice-floes
        through the fat of summer,
                lob-tailing, breaching, sounding,
grazing in the pastures of the sea
        on krill-rich orange plankton
                crackling with life.

You prowled down the continental shelf,
     guided by the sun
         and stars and the taste of alluvial silt
on your way southward
     to the warm lagoons,
         the tropic of desire,
where the lovers lie belly to belly
     in the rub and nuzzle of their sporting;
         and you turned, like a god in exile,
out of your wide primeval element,
     delivered to the mercy of time.
         Master of the whale-roads,
let the white wings of the gulls
     spread out their cover.
         You have become like us,
disgraced and mortal.

About This Story

When we first walked into a local bookshop in Orleans, we asked the owner who he felt the quintessential writers of Cape Cod were. Poet Stanley Kunitz was at the top of his list.

A Pulitzer Prize winner, National Book Award recipient, and former US poet laureate, Kunitz lived to be one hundred and is considered one of the great contemporary poets of our time. Spending his time between New York and Provincetown, Kunitz was a cofounder of the Fine Arts Work Center—where he influenced other writers like Mark Doty, included in this collection   and spent summers on Cape Cod for more than fifty years, tending to his seaside garden. While Kunitz wrote many pieces musing on his time in Provincetown, this poem first published in the *Atlantic Monthly* in 1981 about his encounter with a stranded sixty-three-foot finback whale is one of his most well known and beloved.

Finbacks are a common species of whale around Cape Cod, where they swim and feed, and whale strandings are not an uncommon occurrence. In fact, the Cape is considered a hot spot for cetacean (dolphin and whale) strandings. In 2023, Wellfleet became the site of the largest dolphin stranding event in US history. Over one hundred dolphins were freed by rescuers from multiple organizations who worked tirelessly to direct them back to open water from muddy conditions and "The Gut," a hook-like area of the Cape that experiences extreme tidal fluctuations.

Because these waters have seen significant marine vessel traffic for more than four hundred years, with the region heavily used for maritime shipping to and from the port of Boston, and also serve as a plentiful fishing grounds, it is perhaps inevitable that humans, whales, and other marine life collide here. Many shipwrecks have occurred in this region, as well as many collisions between whales and commercial ships. Still, the Stellwagen Bank National Marine Sanctuary located between Cape Cod and Cape Ann—an 842-square-mile area that is federally protected, kind of like an underwater park—is among the top places in the world to watch whales. The sanctuary was designated as part of the reauthorization of the National Marine Sanctuaries Act signed into law in 1992 in an effort to conserve, protect, and enhance the biological diversity, ecological integrity, and cultural legacies of these places.

When whales like the finback Kunitz witnessed or other marine mammals like dolphins, porpoises, and seals are stranded along the shores of Cape Cod, the Marine Mammal Rescue and Research team of the International Fund for Animal Welfare (IFAW) is deployed to attempt rescue or conduct an investigation and necropsy to look for the cause of the stranding. Strandings have long been attributed to

sick creatures beaching themselves, but the IFAW outlines the various threats caused by humans. "Increased human-inflicted threats
such as underwater noise from ships, collisions with vessels, and
unsustainable fishing practices lead to bycatch and entanglement of
these animals, threatening their ability to communicate, feed, breed,
and survive." Through their efforts, the IFAW is able to help save 80
percent of stranded dolphins and release them back into the wild.

The Ocean's Gifts

LINDA COOMBS

Excerpt from *Colonization and the Wampanoag Story*

The men spent most of their time in the summer at the water, fishing and shellfishing. Strong Bear and Tall Pine took all the boys, River, Woodchuck, and Red Dawn over to the estuary, the mouth of the river. They traveled in two dugout canoes that could each hold three or four people. They built a camp back near the woods, as they would be there for a few days. Smiling Dove and Stands Strong had packed some dry corn and beans for them, as well as some cornmeal. They could gather fresh strawberries, onions and garlic, and lots of new greens for their soups. There were plenty of clams and quahogs, and bass and perch to make a meal a feast! And it was just about the time for the bluefish to run! The boys all looked forward to catching a huge blue to roast over the fire!

Strong Bear and Tall Pine led the boys to the maple swamp. They cut saplings to repair the fish weir that had been built in the estuary. It needed a good number of new upright poles after winter freezes and spring torrents had broken older ones. They peeled the bark and their Dads showed them how to set the poles firmly into the river bottom. This was a lot of work that took most of the day!

They went back to camp, hungry and ready for dinner. Strong Bear, River, and Woodchuck laid out a firepit and got a blaze going. Strong Bear put on a kettle to make soup, and the boys went to collect greens to add to the pot. Tall Pine and Red Down headed one of the boats into open water to look for that bluefish! They had plenty of twisted basswood bark line and newly made fishhooks of deer bone and antler. They also brought along a dip net in case they needed to scoop up a bluefish who was not thrilled with the idea of becoming dinner!

While Tall Pine and Red Dawn were fishing, Woodchuck and River dived into the ocean waves. The salt water was refreshing and relaxing after the hard work of the day! The boys began to feel around the ocean bottom with their feet. It didn't take long to unearth a good number of quahogs to add to tonight's menu. It was low tide when they came out of the water, and they walked along the shore, looking for small holes in the firm sand. Digging at these spots, they added clams to the menu as well. River and Woodchuck could hardly wait to eat! There was nothing like fresh shellfish after the long winter! They looked out and saw Tall Pine and Red Dawn returning with a beautiful bluefish that was almost as long as River's arm. He held his arm against its length (just for accuracy!), always amazed at the sparkling iridescence of the fish's scales glistening in the sunlight.

Tall Pine and Red Dawn gutted the bluefish and put him on a spit. While they were gone, Strong Bear got a good fire going, which now had a big bed of glowing red coals, ready to roast the fish. River and Woodchuck rinsed the sand off the shellfish and put them in a clay kettle and filled it with water. River added a handful of cornmeal to the water to cause the shellfish to spit out any sand they had inside them. Crunchy clams are hard on the teeth!

All the boys helped Strong Bear keep an eye on the bluefish, turning the spit so it would cook evenly. Roasting seemed to take forever to the hungry boys! In actuality, it was nowhere near forever before the fish was almost done. There was just enough time to cook the shellfish—into the soup they went, shells and all, adding their salty flavor.

Finally everything was done! Tall Pine lifted the spit from over the fire, and Red Dawn used the stirring paddle to push the steaming fish into the serving bowl. As the fish cooled, they stood in a circle and gave thanks to all the beings that were now their dinner, grateful for the abundance of food. Everyone filled their own bowls with soup and took a big piece of fish. Woodchuck especially loved the meat that came from the cheeks of the bluefish. It came out in rounds, like little neat treats, two or three bites each.

Both men and boys ate heartily after the long day's work. No one spoke a word for quite a while—not being able to get the food in fast enough!

Before long, though, everyone was full. Strong Bear put away the rest of the fish, saving it for breakfast. The skeleton had a lot of meat left on it and would be a great start to the morning meal. There was no soup or shellfish left at all. Red Dawn washed out the kettle at the shore and set it back on its three stones. His Dad took all the shells a little ways up the beach to dump them into the shell heap. This place had been used as a fish camp for centuries, and everyone always put their shells and bones in the same heap. It was so old that the bottom shells had disintegrated into the earth, and the ones on the surface were bleached by sun and storms and thousands of winters.

Everyone washed his own bowl and spoon. Everyone, that is, except River. He had leaned against one of the frame poles of their shelter and fallen fast asleep—his bowl in his lap and spoon still in his hand. He did get that last bite down before sleep overtook him! Red Dawn washed his dishes, while Tall Pine carried him inside the shelter and laid him on the furs, to continue his journey into dreamland.

Everyone else sat around the fire, talking softly, as the sun began to set. They discussed their plans for fishing and shellfishing over the following days. Smiling Dove, Stands Strong, and the younger girls, Strawberry and Punkinseed, would be coming out in a day or so. They would be smoking and drying most of the clams, quahogs, and mussels that they and the men would be harvesting. They would also preserve some of the fish they caught, to be stored away for winter meals.

The women and girls arrived late the next day, bringing more corn, beans, and cornmeal. They made sleeping areas for themselves and set about making dinner. They had also brought bags of string. Shellfish was cooked and removed from the shell, put on string like a food necklace—only longer—and hung over the fire to smoke. Once completely dried, the fish could last for many months.

Everyone got up early the next day. The women made breakfast while the men went and started digging quahogs, mussels, and clams. They dug for most of the day. Red Dawn and River showed the younger children how to feel out the quahogs with their feet, and to dig clams where the little holes appeared at the shore. The sun was hot on their brown skin, but they could always take a cool dunk in the ocean when needed. Everyone was getting a lot of shellfish! Smiling Dove and Stands Strong steadily steamed them, putting their meat into a large bowl. They showed the younger girls how to string the shellfish and hang them over the smoking racks. When the fires were going good, the women laid dry corncobs on the coals, which would smoke heavily to dry the fish.

Strawberry and Punkinseed each did a few strings, but then decided they had learned enough for one day. They headed for the river, where Punkinseed pointed out a group of little fish. They were using their bodies and tails to sweep away sand in the shallow of the river. Punkinseed explained that they were creating nests where they would lay their eggs and have their babies. She said these fish were called "punkinseeds." Strawberry's eyes widened as she realized they had the same name as her cousin! Her cousin explained that she had gotten that name two years ago, when she had stopped some boys in a canoe from pulling up into a spot where the punkinseeds were laying their eggs.

Strawberry listened intently, seriously taking in her cousin's words. The thought of the boat crushing the fish and obliterating the nests was very disturbing! She was so glad Punkinseed had been able to stop the boat in time!

The girls headed back to camp, where the men had just finished repairing the large net they would use at the weir. The boys were all busy repairing the dip nets with basswood bark cordage. Strawberry and Punkinseed watched them for a while, until the boys asked them to walk down the beach to look for horseshoe crab shells with the tails. When they finished the nets, they would collect thin, straight saplings, first offering some tobacco, cedar, sage, or sweetgrass, or some cornmeal, to pray and give thanks when taking a life. The boys needed saplings that were at least as tall as Red Dawn, trimmed of bark and branches. The horseshoe crab tails would be attached to them with bark string and hide glue, and Red Dawn, Woodchuck, and River would all have new fishing spears!

About This Story

Linda Coombs is an author and historian from the Wampanoag Tribe of Gay Head and the former program director of the Aquinnah Cultural Center. She has emphasized the importance of Wampanoag stories being told by Wampanoag people, and we took her words to heart. Rediscovering Indigenous accounts is always a key part of our process as we build these collections, but one that posed a unique challenge here. Because of diseases introduced by European traders, the Wampanoag were almost completely eradicated just before the Pilgrims arrived.

Facing a pandemic, tribal leaders like Ousamequin and Squanto (also known as Tisquantum) taught the Pilgrims how to plant corn, hunt beaver, and fish, hoping to create allies of the settlers. They brought five deer to the harvest feast now memorialized as Thanksgiving, but it's likely that they weren't actually invited, and the feast was never repeated. Today the Mashpee Wampanoag Tribe observes a National Day of Mourning annually on America's Thanksgiving holiday. The gathering, convened by the United American Indians of New England since 1970, is aimed at educating the public and dispelling myths around the story of this holiday and Indigenous people of the United States.

Wampanoag leaders are working to reclaim their story. Coombs's 2023 book *Colonization and the Wampanoag Story* pictures the tribe before colonization, living in harmony with the abundance of the Cape Cod seashore. The book goes on to give a Wampanoag account that challenges the popular narrative of America's origin story. A new play and pageant entitled *We Are the Land* that tells their story of colonization and resilience debuted in 2023. *We Are the Land* was made by a cast of Wampanoag artists, actors, historians, and storytellers, and Mashpee Wampanoag tribal members Siobhan Brown, Hartman Deetz, and Kitty Hendricks.

Since 1993, the Wôpanâak Language Reclamation Project has sought to return language fluency to the Wampanoag Nation as a principal means of expression. The organization's website shares that the Wampanoag language (Wôpanâôt8âôk) was the first American Indian language to develop and use an alphabetic writing system, primarily due to missionaries arriving from England in the early 1600s to convert the Wampanoag to Christianity. The Wampanoag used this medium not only to communicate with European new-comers but also to record personal letters, wills, deeds, and land transfers, creating the largest body of Native written documents on the continent.

Washing Day in a
Dune Shack

MARY BERGMAN

The parabolic dunes of Provincetown more closely resemble a lunar landscape than any other earthly place. I say this with relative certainty, despite never having traveled to the Moon, or much at all. I have spent the better part of my life in the sand. In October, I lived a week in one of the primitive dune shacks that dot Provincetown's backshore, staring down the Atlantic. No electricity, no running water, and plenty of sand to sweep. There are 19 shacks in total along the three-mile stretch, but this late in the season, all but two or three are unoccupied.

Looking back across the miles of dunes to Provincetown, there are only two manmade indicators that there is bustling town, a tiny heart pulsing, on the other side of the sand. They were built sixty years apart, vastly different in style and function. They are forever linked, serving as port-and-starboard beacons, calling me home.

To the right, jutting above the rise of a foredune, is the Pilgrim Memorial Monument, a quasi-replica of the Torre del Mangia in Siena, Italy, and the tallest all-granite structure in the United

States. As a child, this fact was one of many I would take pride in knowing about our small town, and its relationship to world beyond our shores. The monument was erected between 1907 and 1910 in an ongoing quest to remind the general public that the *Mayflower* first landed in Provincetown, *not* Plymouth. To the left, a 2.7 million gallon water tank, painted sky blue, sits atop a sand dune named for the biblical Mt. Gilboa. It was constructed in 1964 as the town's summer population began to balloon. It serves as a reminder as to why the Pilgrims left Provincetown, only one month after they landed.

Provincetown, for all its natural beauty, history, and freedoms, has no fresh water source of its own. All of the town's drinking water comes from nearby North Truro, miles and miles of pipe snaking under the sand. In November of 1620, after two miserable months at sea, the Pilgrims were in no shape to construct an aqueduct. It was far simpler to pick up and sail across the bay to Plymouth.

It is not surprising that the Pilgrims found no water here, after all, Cape Cod is a sandbar. There is a single underground aquifer that serves as many as 85% of the homes in the fifteen towns that share this elbow of sand. Whatever is spilled onto the sand will eventually leach down into the aquifer—fertilizer, detergents, or, as it happened in 1977, gasoline. An underground gas tank, located just 600 feet from the South Hollow Pumping Station, which provides Provincetown with two-thirds of its water, leaked into the water supply. It took more than three million dollars and eight years before the pumping station could be safely used. Provincetown's population swells from 3,000 to 60,000 or more in the summertime, straining the already delicate water supply. In high summer, when a water-use ban is on, vibrant green lawns and squeaky-clean cars are eyed suspiciously. Though I don't live there anymore, my lawn stays brown in solidarity.

I tell you all this so you can understand the pure joy and wonderment I experienced upon learning that, deep in the sand dunes, some 30 feet below, there is fresh water. All you have to do is dig.

The caretaker shows me how to prime the well, being sure to listen and feel for the pump to catch before a steady stream of unbelievably clear, cool water glug-glugs out of the red metal mouth. I am told I can use all the water I can pump and haul back up the small hill to the shack. In the real world, I have to pay for all the water that comes in and out of the house. My arms are tired, but it is luxurious. On Monday, I wash my clothes by hand in buckets near the well. They snap in the breeze, the only indicator to tourists who have wandered off the path that yes, someone is living here.

On the Pilgrim's first Monday in the New World, the women went ashore for the first time, with the sole purpose of washing clothes. Imagine it: their uneasy steps on dry land, their worn leather shoes sinking into the sand. They praise God that they'd survived the trip, and say a prayer for the two who did not. Then it was time to tackle the task of washing the company's clothes— some 130 people were aboard the *Mayflower*. Their first clean clothes in the New World, starchy with salt from our harbor. They must have strung up a clothesline, wool cloaks and threadbare skirts billowing on deck rails.

I think of these Pilgrim women while I hang my own laundry. From the deck of the cottage, I can make out the pitched roof of a neighboring shack where Harry Kemp, the poet of the dunes, once lived. The so-called "last bohemian," Kemp was also captivated by the Pilgrims, and wanted desperately to give Provincetown her proper due. In 1948, Kemp founded the Provincetown Pilgrims

Association, held reenactments of the first landing and washing day from the Forties until his death in 1960. He traded in his poet's cape for an equally affected costume, some Pilgrim drag complete with buckle hat and musket. He lived in his beach shack, but died, a diabetic and a drunk, in another.

Was that washing day the first time people came to Provincetown to get clean?

My name is Mary, and I'm an alcoholic. I've repeated that refrain so much that the words have lost their power over me, have lost their shame. Mercifully, most of my bad drinking was done far from these shores. I've only gotten drunk in Provincetown once, the last night I spent in our house. Before that, there was the summer we convinced a French exchange student to buy us beer—Coronas, Mike's Hard Lemonade, nothing that was any good or very strong. I remember the Frenchmen because he proudly declared, "I feel like a Kennedy!" as we cruised on a borrowed boat to Long Point, the tip of Cape Cod. I didn't. I never have.

The shack is filled with journal entries of other people's time spent out here. They are dotted, literally and figuratively, with bottles of red and white wine. When I help the women who move in after me, I carry a cardboard box packed so tightly with vodka bottles that they do not make a single sound as I haul them over the sand. There's a Newcastle label inside of the makeshift medicine cabinet, tucked alongside a cracked tube of Neosporin and an ancient bottle of iodine, as if to say, "This elixir, this tincture, will heal you." And maybe it would do the trick for a moment or two, would deaden the silence.

It was not all great-American-novel writing that took place here in the dunes. A large part of the appeal, to hear those who lived it tell it, was that the dunes were a lawless place where you could party, hard. You could get rip-roaring drunk out here, wake

up and dawn and sober up on the two-mile trek over the sand to
your real life.

Laura Fowler, one of the original builders and owners of this
shack, was known for chasing tourists away from her tiny patch of
paradise. She and her husband Stan were dubbed "The Grouches"
by other dune dwellers. I think Laura would have hated to know
someday I, a stranger, would be sitting in her house, drinking from
her well, cooking on her stove, staring at her electrical outlets that
lead to nowhere. Yes, Laura and Stan had the chutzpah to haul a
100-gallon propane tank out over the dunes in their pick-up truck
and hook up a stove, refrigerator, and generator. The wires were
cut, the outlets strange reminders of modern life. They say if Laura
liked you she would invite you inside for a gin and tonic, *on ice*.
It must have been a mirage, a sweltering August day on the sand,
no shade to speak of, to see a woman pulling a tray of ice cubes
out of thin air. It would have been hard to say no to that. Would
I have said no to that?

The sun sets earlier every day. What does it mean to blackout
when it is pitch black from six at night to seven in the morning? I
turn on all the kerosine lamps and I listen to the *Psychedelic Oyster*
radio show. I listen to the radio a lot. I came here for solitude, only
to learn I do not like the sounds of silence. They are the sounds of
the howling wind and the coyotes, each trying to outdo the other.

"My father didn't make it to my college graduation, he was
sailing in Caribbean. So he stopped in a record store and asked
what the new album from the Grateful Dead was, and they put
this on," the DJ drops the needle on *Standing on the Moon*. Inside
this shack, I'm an astronaut, living on a space station anchored
to the uninhabitable surface of some sandy planet, listening to
dispatches from home.

Time, like light, bends differently out here. All the songs are from thirty, forty years ago. I keep the radio on all day. The DJs start taking up space in my head, each crazier than the last.

Here I am in Helltown, here I am on the wild backshore. There are 40 miles of outer beach from Provincetown to Eastham. Every couple of summers, a backpacker or two attempt to follow in the footsteps of Thoreau. I wonder if these guys ever run into each other out there in their quest for seclusion. None of these great men of the dunes were all that alone. Thoreau had an unnamed traveling companion throughout much of *Cape Cod*. Henry Beston hung around the Coast Guard surfmen who patrolled the beach each night. This time of year, it is only me and the seals and the radio station. Even Harry Kemp had friends who would carry him home when he got too drunk to walk.

I don't go to meetings anymore. Maybe I should. The last one I went to was here, in Provincetown, in June. I have meetings with myself now, in coffee shops and, this week, in shacks. I walk over to Harry's shack and open the doors and sit on the wide plank bed where he slept. I tell him I'm sorry that I never liked his poetry much, with too many rhyming couplets. They say your chances of staying sober are much higher if you go to meetings, if you stick with the group. That all you need is two alcoholics talking to each other. What about one alcoholic, talking to ghosts?

Deep in the dunes, there is fresh water running dozens of feet below the sand. There are wells, seemingly unyielding, that tap into these bubbles of water floating just above the salt. In other places, the water springs up in cranberry bogs, in puddles that never dry. If the Pilgrims had found this water, would they have stayed?

By the end of the week, the flowers I picked on washing day have already died. The passing of time, marked in wilted petals. I hope walking barefoot in the sand will smooth over my callouses, will slough off my dead skin and I will be born anew. Failing that, I will take another cold camp shower, my eyes on the horizon, the water tower and the monument and Moon, all rising above me and the dunes.

About This Story

The natural beauty of Cape Cod has long attracted artists, writers, and creative people seeking inspiration or simply a place to escape, focus on their craft, and be alone with their ideas. As an artist colony, this community naturally found a creative use for old outbuildings and guest shacks once used by the US Life-Saving Service and Coast Guard volunteers, then as shelter by Portuguese fishermen. The dune shacks sit on protected national seashore, among the dunes of Truro and Provincetown, and despite being only a couple of miles from the crowds of P-town, they offer, as playwright Eugene O'Neill once described, "a grand place to be alone and undisturbed." Provincetown "washashore" Mary Bergman grew up exploring these dunes in the off-season when the shacks were boarded up against the elements, and she spent a solo week in one of the shacks in October 2017 after being awarded a writing residency there. Her story brings the shack experience to life.

Once under threat of being removed by the government in the transition of this seashore to federal land, these shacks are as much a part of the natural landscape as the dunes they rest upon. They are now protected in the Dune Shacks of Peaked Hill Bars Historic District, a nineteen-hundred-acre tract on the National Register of Historic Places advocated for by long-term seasonal dune dwellers, deemed worthy of preservation for the dune shacks' significant contributions to art and literature in America. The Provincetown

Community Compact maintains and administers the nineteen dune shacks that are part of this historic site, continuing their tradition by offering artist residencies. The Compact describes these shacks as "primitive—no electricity or indoor plumbing—and isolated, allowing for uninterrupted solitude and refuge."

In the summer of 2023, the National Park Service announced plans for a public bid to lease eight of the dune shacks instead of awarding leases to longtime tenants as it had since acquiring the shacks in 1961. This sparked concern from dune dwellers and the people who love the shacks, who saw it as a shortsighted money grab that put historic structures at risk. Robert Wolfe, a cultural anthropologist who conducted a study of the dune shacks, told the *New York Times*, "This is a living piece of American history, a living traditional culture that finds expression in those shacks, and that's lost when you just put random people out there." The Park Service maintains that this action was intended to ensure the shacks' preservation and the integrity of these culturally significant structures.

Harvesting a Return

JARITA DAVIS

Over and over again, owners and overseers of cranberry bogs pronounce the Cape Verder, whether he picks by hand, scoop or snap, the very best harvester of cranberries on the Cape Cod bogs.

—ALBERT JENKS, ANTHROPOLOGIST, 1924

I can look at the cranberries, yes, but not eat them. It's their color that's sweet
when the pink beads and candied crimson pebbles tumble into their wooden boxes.

If you buy your own land, in three to five years you can harvest a full crop.
In three years, I'll be in Fogo again, telling my sobrinahos stories of the bog.

Not about arthritis snapping my hips and ankles as I crouch in the dewy dawn,
or the skin splitting my hand as I reach from the cold, dry air into the wet vines.

I'll bring back different stories, American clothes, and a handful of cranberries
for each child. I'll laugh when they spit the bitter flesh back into their hands.

When their faces gather, scattered brown layers eclipsing each other, I'll tell how here parents
picked and scooped and told children stories of Nho Lobo, the lazy wolf.

How women picked too. Mothers in wide-brimmed hats stained their dresses
while kneeling on crushed leaves and cranberries in the wet bogs, teaching

their children those old Criole songs: the one about the rooster
who longs for his youth, wishing he could fly. And how the children helped,

stumbling under the awkward empty wooden crates, gray and
bigger than themselves, and brought them to their parents, bent in the bogs.

I'll tell them about autumn tumbling behind boxes of cranberries set at the edge of the fields and how the end of each day would fall from the hills with a quiet fire of trees like narrow volcanoes exploding orange and yellow leaves. The evenings folded with the smell of burning wood, as colors collapsed into the sunset.

How all through September and October and November, late into every Saturday night, we sang along with the accordions and mandolins in cabins by the bogs.

We danced, and the children took warm bread with cranberry jam from their mothers' rough hands, hands torn by the berries' vine and stained red beneath the nail.

Work on the bog is work that makes you feel old. Old enough to wonder how you are still bending your back over another man's crops, not your own.

My scoop snaps across the vines' twigs. The money comes slowly, but it comes. Boxes stand stacked, bulging with berries. If the picking is good this year, and next, I'll bring an aching armload of stories and berries back from the fiery fields of this other Cape to those brown faces in the beige mountains of Fogo.

About This Story

Cranberries are a wild fruit native to Cape Cod—they thrive on the region's temperate climate and the acidic, sandy peat soil of the marshes, ponds, and bogs, which can be inundated with water. Cranberries were first harvested by the Wampanoag, and the harvest was industrialized by European settlers in the nineteenth and twentieth centuries, with labor provided by immigrants from Cape Verde, a West African archipelago that has been a Portuguese colony since the 1400s. Cape Verdean "cranberry boggers" were among the first Africans who didn't come to the United States enslaved but as immigrants seeking opportunity. They were descendants of Portuguese colonizers and enslaved people of West Africa, and many of them were drawn to Massachusetts for the promise of its booming whaling industry after the farming industry in Cape Verde suffered from depleted soils and drought.

After the whaling industry collapsed, Cape Verdean-Americans faced discrimination, often denied the same jobs as white Portuguese immigrants. This led them to cranberries, a plentiful crop and an industry in need of laborers. Harvesting cranberries was a physically demanding job with long hours and low pay. Workers were paid by the box rather than the hour, which made an already strenuous job more taxing. Often families picked together along with their children and spent evenings telling stories, playing and dancing to traditional music, and socializing on the bogs.

We were grateful to find Jarita Davis's piece capturing this important history and community unique to Cape Cod in the 2021 collection *From the Farther Shore: Discovering Cape Cod and the Islands Through Poetry*. Her own poetry collection, *Return Flights*, captures Cape Verdean culture shaped by separation and a longing for the home that was left behind.

Provincetown Houses

MARY HEATON VORSE

Excerpt from *Time and the Town: A Provincetown Chronicle*

The very houses are subject to change and move about as though not anchored to the land. In most places when a man builds a house he builds it and there it stands, practically unchanged, keeping the same form in which it began, and almost invariably in the same place. This is not true in Provincetown. Houses there do not remain upon their foundations. Formerly, every summer one saw houses cumbrously moving down the front street.

People in Provincetown do not regard houses as stationary objects. A man will buy a piece of dune land above the town and a cottage on the front shore, and presently up the hill toils the little house. Or he buys a piece of shore front and a cottage on the back street, and presently the house is wambling along to take its place on the water.

It has always been so since the old days. Provincetown people got a habit of moving their houses long ago when there was a settlement of forty-eight houses over by Long Point. This sickle of sand which encloses one of the finest harbors on the North Atlantic was so narrow that encroaching storms played havoc with it and threatened at one time to sweep the narrow point away. It was too valuable a harbor to be destroyed and the government took it over. But the thrifty Provincetowners asked the government:

"What are you going to do with these houses?"

"Nothing," responded the government.

"Well, can we take them?"

"If you take them away," answered the government. The Provincetown fathers consulted together. And next, houses supported on wrecking barrels bobbed solemnly across the bay. They "figgered" it this way.

If wrecking barrels can support and bring up from the sea's bottom a vessel of many tons' burden, why can't a raft of wrecking barrels support a house on the surface of the water? It could and did. Arnold's Radio Shop, formerly Matheson's Department Store, then our principal store in town, was once the schoolhouse, and though a large building it went to sea and became an amphibious animal. They say that so gently were these houses eased off that the moving didn't interfere with the housewife cooking her dinner.

It is not only from Long Point that houses have moved. The old records show that there was once a considerable village on Beach Point. Long ago all these houses were hauled away. Some were moved to Provincetown and others to Truro.

There was also a settlement known as Hell Town, between Wood End and Race Point; of this not a vestige remained. When people no longer needed to fish on the outside shore because of the coming of motors, these houses were moved into town. I asked Captain Kennedy, a neighbor of mine, why they called this settlement Hell Town.

"Because of the helling that went on there," he answered, simply. . . .

Provincetown men are not landsmen. Almost without exception they have at one time or another "followed the sea." Certainly their forebears have. Provincetowners have spent so much of their time on the sea in ships that they look upon houses as a sort of land ship or a species of houseboat and therefore not subject to the laws of houses.

Every man who owns a boat or a vessel overhauls it, alters it, tinkers with it. That is why all Provincetown people tinker with their houses and keep adding to them perpetually. The people here are seafaring folk and that is why carpentry on houses is never done and why the houses do not stay upon their foundations after the fashion of those in other towns but go wandering up roadways of sandy dunes.

Many a ship's timber has gone into Provincetown houses. Some have been partly constructed from the fine knees of old vessels and the magnificent timbers of dead ships. Frederick Waugh's studio was made that way and the interesting Flagship owes much of its uniqueness to Pat's beachcombing. This likeness of Provincetown houses to ships explains some of their architectural peculiarities. In many an old house the door opens on a narrow entry. The stairs mount sheer. They are not really stairs but a companion-way. There are upper chambers where the small windows are like portholes, as though built for security against the weather rather than for light.

When the Winslows bought a piece of property near us and went to build a new house there, the question was what to do with the old house. The carpenter was a Provincetown man and he was not for a moment perplexed. He rolled the old house out into the bay and there he anchored it. A storm came up and for two days the distracted house rocked and curtsied. Its shutters and doors blew open and the blank windows and the yawning door looked like a doleful screaming mouth.

One day Tony Avellar shouted to me, "Want to come and tow a house over to Beach Point?"

He hitched his gas boat to the house and slowly we chugged and bobbed across the Bay, where men rolled the house across the beach, and there it became a garage.

George O'Neill, the poet, and his mother were looking for a house to buy and found one in Wellfleet. It was a lovely house, remote behind a hedge of lilacs. Yet this house, in some ghostly fashion, resisted their buying. Keys, when they wished to go in, would be lost. Furniture moved so they stumbled over it. They had a curious sense of being unwanted as they walked through the house they coveted. After a number of disquieting episodes they left the house alone awhile. But they could not stop wanting the old Cape Cod house behind the lilacs. I drove with them to look at it again.

We got to the lilac hedge, but there was no house at all. They were sure this was the place where the house was, but there were only scattered plaster and a few bricks, and the place where the house once had been was overgrown with summer weeds.

We thought we had taken a wrong road. We searched until some old neighbors told us the house had been bought back by relatives of its former owners, and, as the old people said, "had gone to Chatham." It was as though this house had slyly evaded intruders until its own family had come for it. . . .

Houses in Provincetown are still restless and movable. One of the latest houses to wander around is the old Pamet Coast Guard

Station which was bought by the Marx', cut into sections, and moved from its niche on the shore to the hills above where there is a magnificent view. And only the other day Mr. Chipman, the house mover, died while he was moving five cottages from inland to the shore.

The Back Country

MARY HEATON VORSE

Excerpt from *Time and the Town: A Provincetown Chronicle*

I

During this time there were two escapes from the young confusion of the house. One was out on the water and the other was the back country. I don't know any other place where the wild country is so close to a town. You can walk out of your door on the back street into it.

I would leave the town behind me, plunge into the woods, cross the railway track, and go up the Atkins Mayo Road, up a steep sand hill, and then turn right into a trail, scarcely visible between blueberry bushes, which we called the Little Trail. This was the shortest road to the dunes. The trail cut through the blueberry moors, dipped into pine woods, and arrived in a little valley where the light filtered through the green leaves of young trees. Wild lilies of the valley were underfoot. The green from above and that underfoot made one feel as if one were in some magical atmosphere between air and water. The dunes came down sharply and there was a swift ascent through the tops of wild cherries and gnarled beach plum bushes.

Suddenly the dunes spread their majestic immensity before one—beyond them, the blue line of ocean. The only sign that man had ever been here was far off the top of Peaked Hill Bars station appearing behind a high dune. I would sit there and the quiet of dune and sea and sky would pour over me and heal me from the new, bewildering world.

Often I went over to the station, or swam on the outside shore. Sometimes I would only stop on the dune's edge, and one of the coast guard would say to me reproachfully, "Saw you on the edge of the dunes yesterday from the watchtower. Was expecting you over. Why didn't you come?"

Although it has been a long time since I was at Peaked Hill, I still feel as if there were an invisible path between that far station on the outside dunes and our house, so often have I crossed to it.

Sometimes when I couldn't sleep, I would go out through the back country at night. I knew the trails so well that I was night-footed and would let my feet take me, trusting them to find the way up the dunes and sit and watch dawn break.

The back country is like a wild little animal that crouches under the hand of man but is never tamed. It has been left to grow wild generation by generation since the time when people were forbidden to pasture sheep and cattle for fear of the encroaching sand.

The woods of scrub pines are all trees of second growth. The moors that are covered with blueberry and wild cranberry have little trails made by Indians or by animals going to forgotten water holes. There are few people who know the dunes well enough to leave these trails, for on one hand there are entanglements of bull brier that only a machete could cut, and on the other hand unpassable marsh in your way. People have become hopelessly lost in the back country and have had their clothes torn from them by briers or been bogged to the waist trying to cross a treacherous marsh.

II

Once on a snowy day we went out to the dunes and came back by
the Atkins Mayo Road. In the snow were fresh tracks of a wheelbarrow and feet which suddenly began in the middle of the dune.
Someone must have pushed this wheelbarrow from the back side
and then the tracks were blown away by the wind and snow. We
followed the tracks, wondering why anyone in winter should
push a wheelbarrow through this wild country and what he had
found in the back shore that would make this work valuable. The
wheelbarrow track followed the Atkins Mayo Road for a time, then
branched to the left and came to the railway cut. The railway cut is
sixty feet high. Right to the edge of this high precipice went the foot
tracks and the track of the wheelbarrow, and then they vanished.
There were no signs of feet going down the perpendicular side and
there were no signs on the sand that had blown across the track.

There was never any answer as to how that wheelbarrow flew
through the air or what it was doing on the back country. It was
one of the many mysteries of the back country and the dunes to
which there is no answer.

The mystery of the wheelbarrow had for a companion piece
the mystery of the kitchen stove. We walked over to Peaked
Hill Bars at least two or three times a week. One day as we were
walking across, we saw a black spot. It was quite a way to the
left of the Snail Road. We went up to see what it was. It was a
kitchen stove in good repair. There it sat for no reason at all, near
no road, near no wagon track, a fine kitchen stove. There also it
remained year by year and rusted away and the sands covered
it. You can be puzzled by the hour as to why or what brought
the kitchen stove. Sinclair Lewis made a legend about it. He
said that one of the wives of the lifeguards got mad and left for

home and, naturally, took her stove along and didn't notice till
too late that it was gone. He pointed out that that was the only
way that a kitchen stove could have got there unless an airplane
had dropped it, which seemed unlikely.

III

I do not know of any country which is so wild and so diverse within
so small a compass. This little piece of land, small when you measure it in square miles, is unlike any other place; nor have I found
anyone who has seen anything like it.

In the fall the sweep of its color is incredible. Then the moors
are washed with purple of the wild cranberries. The blueberries
and blackberries are scarlet. In some places the wild country leads
down to the orange-colored salt marshes, and the maples around
the edges of ponds turn scarlet and the bull brier are plates of
gold. The whole back country is spicy with bay and sweet fern.

In the spring there is a bloom of wild fruit which spreads like
a bridal veil of shad and juicy pear and wild cherries and beach
plum, growing in great quantities where the dunes and the woods
meet. The high dunes over by Mayflower Heights are dappled
with white in the spring.

All through the season there are blueberries and huckleberries.
Later the high bush blueberries ripen near the swamps. Every
season of the year there are berries to pick, from the wild strawberries through blueberry and huckleberry time, till fall when
one goes wild grapin' and beach plummin'. The last fruit of all, is
the cranberry; all through the back country are little wild bogs of
cranberries that have planted themselves or that someone once
planted and let go wild.

The Cape is dotted with secret ponds, one after another. Shank
Painter Pond which is shrinking to a marsh has water lilies and

floating islands. Around these ponds on the shore one will often find the sharp, delicate tracks of deer.

They are all stocked with fish. Carp, bass, and perch are plentiful and no one troubles to fish them. Some of the fishermen used to take a busman's holiday and put on hip boots and come back with strings of fine fish. At Herring River up Wellfleet way, there are trout.

The back country is so wild that it abounds with little creatures. Many of them, like the rabbits and puff adders and toads, have turned dune color. Foxes slide through the underbrush. There is a man in Provincetown who traps him a score of foxes every winter. Formerly when I used to go up the little trail I often raised a covey of quail. They would erupt almost under my feet and go whirring past me.

The beach grass makes beautiful circles on the dunes. The patterns are so lovely that wonderful photographs have been made of them. The little dune mice feed on the grass and at the edge of the dunes there is a complicated pattern of the feet of the wild things, and finer traceries yet of the insects which also are dune-colored.

There were foot tracks that we could recognize, of squirrel, coon, rabbit, and of turtle, who drag their tails when they walk, and there were other foot tracks we couldn't recognize at all. The legend is that there are ghost animals left by the Indians. We would divide the tracks into those of regular animals and those of irregular animals, the ghost tracks of non-existent creatures of a distant day. Some times inland on the dunes there would be enormous bird tracks we could not recognize.

Once down the steep side of a dune we found a track as though of a large ball. It ended suddenly. There were no foot prints leading to it or going away from it and there was no ball. It was the track of some large thing that had rolled.

IV

The dunes have many legends. One of the first that I heard was of the white stallion. Many years ago there was a vessel bound for Nova Scotia, with a cargo of fine horses and cattle, wrecked off Peaked Hill Bars. All were drowned but a beautiful white stallion who swam ashore. For a year he ran wild up and down the dunes, the most beautiful creature that one could imagine. Many people tried to catch him and bait him with oats or trap him in various ways but always he went free again and galloped the dunes to his own liking. Then they made an enclosure and brought a mare and he went to the mare. When he found he was trapped the fury of the free filled him. He threw himself against the palings again and again. The dunes resounded to his neigh and the pounding of his angry hoofs.

At last, as though he had wings he sailed over the high enclosure. But two lines of men were stretched out over the dunes. He ran from them and stood on the top of a dune, his great figure with its white mane silhouetted against the evening sky. As the men again approached him on both sides, only escape by sea was possible. He saw his pursuers to right and to left, as he stood pawing the sand. Then as a man with a rope approached him, he reared his head and plunged furiously into the sea. They could see his white mane tossing above the water as he swam on out and out, defying them to capture him and preferring death to captivity. When I first came here the old coast guard still spoke of the waves as white horses.

About These Stories

Mary Heaton Vorse's 1942 book *Time and the Town: A Provincetown Chronicle* is a classic Cape Cod read, capturing life as it was in Provincetown from her first summer there in 1906 to her death in 1966 at age ninety-one. Provincetown was a fitting place for somebody as progressive as Vorse, and she felt at home living among artists, writers, playwrights, intellectuals, and radicals also drawn to this peculiar town on the edge of the sea. She was a prominent figure in social justice movements—protesting for the rights of women, laborers, and immigrants—and in journalism, covering the Lawrence textile strike of 1912, the Ludlow Massacre in 1914 in Colorado, the Great Steel Strike of 1919, and the 1937 autoworkers' strike and factory takeover in Flint, Michigan. When she wasn't reporting, she was capturing musings about her life on Cape Cod. Her essays in *Time and the Town* highlight her own connection to this place and, no surprise, at times convey a journalistic view of the history, politics, and economics of this place.

We were thrilled to happen upon her essay "Provincetown Houses" after a local first clued us in to this peculiar bit of Cape Cod history. The more we visited life-saving stations, lighthouses, and other structures that had been moved from one place to another, the more we pondered if this region can serve in a time of climate change as a model of resiliency and adaptability—or perhaps just stubbornness in not accepting the dynamic realities of beloved environments. In either case, we appreciate the resourcefulness of Cape Codders and admire Vorse's ability to ground us through a glimpse into local ways, lore, and observations from this place she held so dear.

To preserve her cultural legacy and save her home from disrepair (or worse, developers), Vorse's granddaughters enlisted the help of neighbors Ken Fulk, a designer, and his husband, Kurt Wootton, who purchased the home and brought it back to life as a community asset and gathering place. The Vorse House embodies her spirit and history by welcoming artists, writers, and creatives through artist residencies, events, and art exhibitions.

Humpbacks

MARY OLIVER

There is, all around us,
this country
of original fire.

You know what I mean.

The sky, after all, stops at nothing, so something
   has to be holding
   our bodies
in its rich and timeless stables or else
we would fly away.

✦

Off Stellwagen
off the Cape,
the humpbacks rise. Carrying their tonnage
   of barnacles and joy
they leap through the water, they nuzzle back under it
like children
at play.

✦

They sing, too.
And not for any reason
you can't imagine.

✦

Three of them
rise to the surface near the bow of the boat,
then dive
deeply, their huge scarred flukes
tipped to the air.

We wait, not knowing
just where it will happen; suddenly
they smash through the surface, someone begins
shouting for joy and you realize
it is yourself as they surge
upward and you see for the first time
how huge they are, as they breach,
and dive, and breach again
through the shining blue flowers
of the split water and you see them
for some unbelievable
part of a moment against the sky—
like nothing you've ever imagined—
like the myth of the fifth morning galloping
out of darkness, pouring
heavenward, spinning; then

✦

they crash back under those black silks
and we all fall back

together into that wet fire, you
know what I mean.

✦

I know a captain who has seen them
playing with seaweed, swimming
through the green islands, tossing
the slippery branches into the air.

I know a whale that will come to the boat whenever
she can, and nudge it gently along the bow
with her long flipper.

I know several lives worth living.

✦

Listen, whatever it is you try
to do with your life, nothing will ever dazzle you
like the dreams of your body,

its spirit
longing to fly while the dead-weight bones
toss their dark mane and hurry
back into the fields of glittering fire

where everything,
even the great whale,
throbs with song.

About This Story

It was Cape Cod that inspired much of the work of Mary Oliver, the beloved poet of nature, winner of the Pulitzer Prize in 1984 and the National Book Award in 1992. With roots in Ohio, Oliver moved to Provincetown in the 1960s to live with her longtime love, Molly Malone Cook, who opened an art gallery and later a bookstore. Contrary to the image of many great nature writers—off alone in a cabin in the woods—Oliver was well known around town, friendly and chatty with locals, though she was immensely private. She called this town home for more than fifty years and, like many prominent writers associated with Provincetown, was involved with the Fine Arts Work Center. She became one of its first faculty members and established the fellowship program that to this day provides writers with a place to live and write; many of whom go on to distinguished, award-winning careers.

Locals could count on Mary, as constant as the tides, walking along the beach on the edge of town in the early mornings, or taking hours-long walks through the Province Lands. Her observations on these walks—particularly along the edges of the Cape, along the then newly established national seashore, among dunes, pitch pines, marshland, and ponds—fueled much of her work. Mary Oliver is *our* Thoreau, so we wanted to follow in her footsteps on our visit. At Blackwater Pond in mid-autumn, we nearly immediately felt a deeper connection with her writing. The glowing golden landscape that inspired some of her most memorable lines in her poem "In Blackwater Woods" invited introspection.

But it was this poem found in her 2010 collection *The Truro Bear and Other Adventures* focused away from land that felt uniquely Cape Cod, capturing the exuberance and thrill of bearing witness to whales. On our visit, we tagged along on a private chartered boat with educator and writer Elizabeth Bradfield. Liz has gone out as an educator on whale watch boats with throngs of tourists multiple times a week for decades, and she was giddy with information and familiarity with the whales who visited us during our three hours on unusually calm waters. On a late October afternoon, we oohed and aahed in harmony, stood with clownlike grins staring in wonderment at these giant and gentle creatures, and laughed at times from the pure joy of it all—of simply being in their presence.

Cape Cod

HENRY DAVID THOREAU

Excerpt from *Cape Cod*

It was one of the hottest days in the year, yet I found the water so icy cold that I could swim but a stroke or two, and thought that, in case of shipwreck, there would be more danger of being chilled to death than simply drowned. One immersion was enough to make you forget the dog-days utterly. Though you were sweltering before, it will take you half an hour now to remember that it was ever warm. There were the tawny rocks, like lions couchant, defying the ocean, whose waves incessantly dashed against and scoured them with vast quantities of gravel. The water held in their little hollows, on the receding of the tide, was so crystalline that I could not believe it salt, but wished to drink it; and higher up were basins of fresh water left by the rain, — all which, being also of different depths and temperature, were convenient for different kinds of baths. Also, the larger hollows in the smoothed rocks formed the most convenient of seats and dressing-rooms. In these respects it was the most perfect seashore that I had seen.

I saw in Cohasset, separated from the sea only by a narrow beach, a handsome but shallow lake of some four hundred acres, which, I was told, the sea had tossed over the beach in a great storm in the spring, and, after the alewives had passed into it, it had stopped up its outlet, and now the alewives were dying by thousands, and the inhabitants were apprehending a pestilence as the water evaporated. It had five rocky islets in it.

This rocky shore is called Pleasant Cove, on some maps; on the map of Cohasset, that name appears to be confined to the particular cove where I saw the wreck of the *St. John*. The ocean did not look, now, as if any were ever shipwrecked in it; it was not grand and sublime, but beautiful as a lake. Not a vestige of a wreck was visible, nor could I believe that the bones of many a shipwrecked man were buried in that pure sand. . . .

Yet this same placid Ocean, as civil now as a city's harbor, a place for ships and commerce, will erelong be lashed into sudden fury, and all its caves and cliffs will resound with tumult. It will ruthlessly heave these vessels to and fro, break them in pieces in its sandy or stony jaws, and deliver their crews to sea-monsters. It will play with them like sea-weed, distend them like dead frogs, and carry them about, now high, now low, to show to the fishes, giving them a nibble. This gentle Ocean will toss and tear the rag of a man's body like the father of mad bulls, and his relatives may be seen seeking the remnants for weeks along the strand. From some quiet inland hamlet they have rushed weeping to the unheard-of shore, and now stand uncertain where a sailor has recently been buried amid the sandhills.

It is generally supposed that they who have long been conversant with the Ocean can foretell by certain indications, such as its roar and the notes of sea-fowl, when it will change from calm to storm; but probably no such ancient mariner as we dream of exists; they know no more, at least, than the older sailors do about this voyage of life on which we are all embarked. Nevertheless, we love to hear the sayings of old sailors, and their accounts of natural phenomena, which totally ignore, and are ignored by, science; and possibly they have not always looked over the gunwale so long in vain. . . .

The sea-shore is a sort of neutral ground, a most advantageous point from which to contemplate this world. It is even a trivial place. The waves forever rolling to the land are too far-travelled and untamable to be familiar. Creeping along the endless beach amid the sun-squall and the foam, it occurs to us that we, too, are the product of sea-slime.

It is a wild, rank place, and there is no flattery in it. Strewn with crabs, horse-shoes, and razor-clams, and whatever the sea casts up, — a vast *morgue*, where famished dogs may range in packs, and crows come daily to glean the pittance which the tide leaves them. The carcasses of men and beasts together lie stately up upon its shelf, rotting and bleaching in the sun and waves, and each tide turns them in their beds, and tucks fresh sand under them. There is naked Nature, inhumanly sincere, wasting no thought on man, nibbling at the cliffy shore where gulls wheel amid the spray. . . .

Most persons visit the sea-side in warm weather, when fogs are frequent, and the atmosphere is wont to be thick, and the charm of the sea is to some extent lost. But I *suspect* that the fall is the best season, for then the atmosphere is more transparent, and it is a greater pleasure to look out over the sea. The clear and bracing air, and the storms of autumn and winter even, are necessary in order that we may get the impression which the sea is calculated to make. In October, when the weather is not intolerably cold, and the landscape wears its autumnal tints, such as, methinks, only a Cape Cod landscape ever wears, especially if you have a storm during your stay, — that I am convinced is the best time to visit this shore. In autumn, even in August, the thoughtful days begin, and we can walk anywhere with profit. Beside, an outward cold and dreariness, which make it necessary to seek shelter at night, lend a spirit of adventure to a walk.

The time must come when this coast will be a place of resort for those New-Englanders who really wish to visit the sea-side. At present it is wholly unknown to the fashionable world, and probably it will never be agreeable to them. If it is merely a ten-pin alley, or a circular railway, or an ocean of mint-julep, that the visitor is in search of, — if he thinks more of the wine than the brine, as I suspect some do at Newport, — I trust that for a long time he will be disappointed here. But this shore will never be more attractive than it is now. Such beaches as are fashionable are here made and unmade in a day, I may almost say, by the sea shifting its sands. Lynn and Nantasket! this bare and bended arm it is that makes the bay in which they lie so snugly. What are springs and waterfalls? Here is the spring of springs, the waterfall of waterfalls. A storm in the fall or winter is the time to visit it; a light-house or a fisherman's hut the true hotel. A man may stand there and put all America behind him.

About This Story

Back at a time when Cape Cod was more fishing wharf than vacation destination, Thoreau was one of its first tourists, not here to hunt but just to get away. Between 1849 and 1855, he made three separate trips to Cape Cod, to "get a better view than I had yet had of the ocean."

He had just spent twenty-six months at Walden Pond between 1845 and 1847, and it was while he was writing the book that would make his career that Thoreau took a few excursions to the beach. Unlike *Walden* with its philosophical and contemplative introspection, *Cape Cod* takes a more naturalist approach—capturing Thoreau's observations in unemotional descriptive prose, documenting the region's environment and its people in a way that admittedly can be quite dry at times. Despite this, Thoreau's importance to the region endures, and his contributions to the cultural landscape of Cape Cod are intertwined with its physical landscape.

Thoreau's Cape Cod writings, published first as chapters in the magazine *Putnam's Monthly* and then collected in a book published in 1865, introduced Americans to the beauty and uniqueness of this landscape—which over time influenced the idea of the Cape as a vacation destination. Soon after, the Cape saw the development of railroads and resort hotels, and began to welcome camps of religious groups, businessmen, and hunting or sporting groups. By the 1870s, summer tourism at the Cape had kicked into high gear. More than anything else, Thoreau's documentation of this place and the landscape that continues to provide solitude and inspiration have made the Cape a destination for writers.

Throughout much of the Cape Cod material we read and in the campfire stories we chose to include here, we saw authors grappling with the legacy of Thoreau in their own writing and reflecting on how the landscape has changed from what he described in his travelogue. Some continue to build on the tradition of writers here, and some literally follow in Thoreau's footsteps. Can writing make you love a place? In Thoreau's case, it did.

Following Thoreau

DAVID GESSNER

Excerpt from *A Wild, Rank Place*

"Oh, you're doing the Thoreau thing?"

He is a plump little man, balding, with small patches of orange hair. He works as a ranger at the Cape Cod National Seashore, but from the looks of him he never gets out from behind his desk. He asks his question dismissively, with an air of superiority.

Yes, I admit, I want to follow Thoreau's route up the outside of the Cape. Doing the Thoreau thing makes it sound like some sort of dance, and the idea of the hike, which I thought so original just a minute ago, now seems tired. I picture hordes of us, Thoreau wannabes—individualists all—marching out over the dunes.

"It's a hard walk, you know."

He says this sternly and looks me up and down, deciding whether or not I'm up to it. That's better. Maybe I imagined the condescension. I lift up my backpack and assure him that I've done a good deal of camping in the West. He nods and helps me plot the trip on my map. By the time I leave he seems genuinely interested in my journey. He points me out to a fellow ranger.

"This guy's going to do the Thoreau trip," he brags.

Well, not exactly. Thoreau started his journey in Concord. I plan to hike from Eastham to Provincetown, taking three days as Thoreau did. Henry called it a "leisurely walk." We'll see. . . .

I like myself best when I'm hiking. This I think as I churn up the beach. A romantic thought, of course. Really what I'm doing is somewhat repetitive and painful—carrying a backpack through deep sand as the straps cut into my shoulders, looking out at a scene of beach and ocean I've seen a thousand times before. But I'm happy, stupidly so, for whatever reason.

While some parts of the Cape have filled up with Dairy Queens and 7-11s, here there are no stores and few houses. Like Thoreau, I stick to the "backside of the Cape." On my left loom cliffs of sand with red clay streaks, to my right lies the Atlantic. It doesn't take long to realize the advantage of taking my shoes off and hiking close to the water, where the sand is hard and more firm. I try to avoid the orange blotches of jellyfish that dot the shore. It's an uneven sort of hike—one leg up higher than the other—not a "tramp-tramp" but more a "tramp-sludge-tramp-sludge," like a soldier with a wounded leg.

The waves set a cadence for my march. That's the paradox here, the constancy of the waves and the flux of the shore, water constantly sculpting land. After a while I hike up closer to the dunes and walk through the kelp beds, hundreds of black flies shooting off before my steps. The beach's yard sale is full today: an old laundry basket, detergent jugs, chunks of green Styrofoam, a trash can, a tangled green net, and dozens of pieces of driftwood twisted in dead-steer shapes.

It turns out that by walking closer to the dunes I intrude on another's turf. Terns, nesting nearby, go on the alert. They ward me off, circling, screeching, making a show of it, while their off-spring scoot behind them, no bigger than plovers. The terns are wonderful fliers, with sleek bullet bodies like living check marks and swallow-type wings. Even running they're aerodynamic, tucking their heads low like bike racers.

I see human fauna, too. A band of surfers lying on the beach in black wet suits look like a gathering of seals. In their midst is one girl in cutoff dungarees and a black bikini top. The top pushes her breasts up and in, a white rim of flesh circumnavigating the black. I feel my shoulders go back and my pace quicken, moving with stronger strides until the group is far behind.

It's a clear day in late spring and I walk without a shirt though I know I'll burn. I read recently in one of my father's cancer books that lying out in the sun is like lying beside a nuclear reactor. But while the scientists tell us the sun is our enemy, I can't help holding on to older, healthier associations. Two Junes ago I had daily doses of another kind of radiation. After treatment I felt like I was driving around on the back of a bus drinking cheap beer—extreme nausea the entire month. I insist that this, the sun's radiation, is different. It makes me feel whole, healthy, full.

I've found my rhythm now. Chomping a carrot, enjoying the mindless physical exertion, breathing in and out to the beat of the waves. What a joyful thing locomotion can be! Though I swore I would take a three-day vacation from worrying about him, I find myself thinking about my father. He can no longer feel the simple physical pleasure of moving, of swinging his arms and walking and breathing without pain. I walk for him, too. . . .

Later that day, coming back from the beach, I spotted a rabbit. The rabbit twitched its nose, sensed me, froze. I padded quietly up behind an old, deeply carved locust tree. While the rabbit stared out with its black eyes and tapped its foot nervously, I readied my weapon. I curled my fingers around the sandy, dog-chewed plastic. I crouched like an Indian, my eyes bored into the gray-and-black-speckled pelt as I screwed myself up into a tight knot. Ten, fifteen seconds passed. I tensed my body. Then, with an abrupt, violent jerk, I sent the Frisbee spinning toward its warm-blooded target.

I wonder what I would have done with a rabbit corpse. Eaten it raw? Cooked it on a spit? Charged at it and sunk my teeth into its fury neck? Fortunately the Frisbee missed, or I'd likely have broken into a fit of blubbering apology, hugging the poor creature to my chest and blurting "sorry" after "sorry." Of course, I was really plagiarizing, not hunting. By day I read of Thoreau's urge to mug a woodchuck. By night I tried to murder rabbits.

I hike up at Cahoon Hollow Beach. At first the trees are stunted just as Thoreau described, but as I walk inland, by Great Pond, they grow taller, much taller than any he wrote of. The Cape of today looks more like it did two hundred years before Thoreau than like Thoreau's Cape. When the Pilgrims arrived they spoke of the fine soil and varied woods, but Henry saw a much more barren land, spotted occasionally with "scrubby wood." The Cape was one of America's first and most graphic examples of industry destroying an environment. Those industries were shipbuilding and the salt works—huge wooden vats where salt was gathered when seawater evaporated. Together they stripped the land of trees.

Thoreau called my town, Dennis, "exceedingly barren and desolate country." These days a wild moat of briars, bayberry, fruit trees, oak, locust, and pine surrounds my house, and it wasn't too long ago I saw the coyote dipping into the bushes below our property. "Yet there were deer here once," Thoreau wrote. Three mornings ago I surprised two deer that had climbed down to the beach at low tide. Despite all the development, in some ways today's Cape is closer to what we consider wild than Thoreau's. . . .

· ✦ ·

After an hour or so I climb through an opening in the cliffs, emerging at a small pond surrounded by a thick beard of poison ivy. The lip of the cliff provides relief—walking on even, firmer land. I now hike atop what Thoreau called "the backbone of the Cape." A hundred feet above the beach, moving at a giant's pace, I look down at two people-dots below. I think of Maushop, the gentle giant of Wampanoag legend. "In the beginning there was nothing but seawater on top of land," I read in *The Narrow Land*, my book of Cape myths. "Much water, much fog." Not long after that, after Kehtean formed the earth and the people, drowning them once for good measure before re-creating them, Maushop came along. Maushop dug Scargo Lake in Dennis, and formed Martha's Vineyard and Nantucket by emptying the sand out of his moccasins. And it was Maushop who saved the Wampanoag people from the evil bird-monster and who became their great friend and protector. Finally, though, the Pukwudgee-the evil pygmies who lived in the reeds in the marshes betrayed Maushop. Alone they couldn't defeat him, but together they blinded his sons and finally drove him from the Cape.

Of course, I belabor the obvious by pointing out that pygmies still run the Cape. Instead of giants, more and more of us—smaller and smaller—crowd each other out as we fill up what the Wampanoag called "the narrow land." And the land *is* narrow, far too narrow to hold so many of us, no matter how small. . . .

· ✦ ·

"A thousand men could not have interrupted the vastness," Thoreau said of the Cape. Could he have imagined ten thousand? A hundred thousand? Henry, I'm sad to be the one to tell you, but the vastness can—and has been—interrupted. Could you have possibly predicted the thousands of cars that herd back and forth across the bridge every Friday and Sunday evening? Could you even have imagined cars, each spitting its weight in poison into the atmosphere? Faster and faster, more and more.

Some things you couldn't have begun to guess. Swimming among used syringes and sewage, for instance. Or all the tumorous homes bulging from your barren Cape. Since your time we've been forced into smaller and smaller plots. When old man Stone moved to East Dennis in the early part of the twentieth century, he bought the entire neck for nothing. Now each tiny plot is worth a fortune. Even as late as 1960 the Cape still felt like a series of frontier towns, and you could have bought our whole neighborhood for the current price of one house. Today I'd need to be a wealthy man to be able to buy a plot considered undersized just thirty years ago.

It's the way of our time. Maushop dies while the pygmies proliferate. I should know, Henry—I speak to you as pygmy to giant. In the same way Stone claimed Sesuit neck, you, in one casually written, posthumously published book—a book far from a masterpiece—laid claim to the entire Cape.

Early men and women are by nature pioneers, and those who come later explore the explored. While older writers claim huge swaths of land, we now go about cultivating our smaller, limited plots. As I sit down to eat lunch and do my daily reading, I find that I have again plagiarized; this morning I crossed the Cape almost exactly where Thoreau did a hundred and forty-seven years ago. I thought I'd chosen my own route this one time, but I followed him despite myself.

This brings home the irony of my entire trip. How do I justify "doing the Thoreau thing?" In following someone who was never a follower, in making an icon of an iconoclast? Why hero-worship a man who counseled men to be their own heroes? I laugh at my convolutions. The very fact of my writing this essay is due to Thoreau, since he practically created the genre in America. But then he didn't write to fit a genre; he wrote and the genre fit him. . . .

And so, Henry, over the years I have tried to learn by reading and emulating you. And by following you I've learned lessons of discipline, self-reliance, appreciation of nature, and open-mindedness. I've done things I never would have done without you, like taking this trip. For that I thank you.

That said, I'm now thinking that the time has come to remove your picture from the wall above my desk. I'm sick of following you. I'd like to take my next trip to an unfamiliar place I haven't read about, and that I won't write about either. Or, if I do end up writing about it, I'd like to do so without the funhouse mirror reflections of past writers and writings.

I've been too deferential to my own heroes, too afraid to topple statues. Emerson wrote of meek young men in libraries, believing it is their duty to accept the views which Cicero, which Locke, which Bacon, have given; forgetful that Cicero, Locke, and Bacon were only young men in libraries when they wrote these books.

I've been one of those meek young men. I've been too polite, but now I'm ready for my extended adolescence to end. After all, fatherlessness is a condition we all eventually have to accept, and which I'll know about soon. Time to thank these heroes, Thoreau first and foremost, for what they've given me and then move beyond. Of course, I'll still be following Thoreau. What could be more like him than taking a path of my own?

About This Story

More than a century and a half later, David Gessner walks in the shadow of Henry David Thoreau with each step he takes along the shores of Cape Cod. Thoreau didn't make his reputation with *Cape Cod*, which is regarded as a lesser work. That honor belongs to *Walden*. So it is not a masterwork that others seek to follow when they embark on "the Thoreau trip." It is, in fact, chasing the *legacy* of a man who declared, "All nature is my bride," and whose more scientific and realistic writing would challenge the Transcendentalists of his time and lay a groundwork for the way we think about the natural world today.

Gessner is the author of thirteen books and a professor of creative writing at the University of North Carolina, Wilmington. We chose to focus this excerpt on his observations along Thoreau's path, making clear the stark differences between Gessner's contemporary Cape Cod and that of Thoreau so long ago. But in the original text, he intersperses these observations with a reflection on his lifelong relationship with Thoreau, having first read him as a sophomore in high school and revisited his work again and again. Gessner confronts the shadow of his hero and learns to step out on his own, just as Cape Cod has done—reinventing itself over and over as it has morphed from what Thoreau once called "a wild, rank place" with "no flattery in it" into the place with the reputation it enjoys today.

Learning to
Live with Water

ADELINE CARRIE KOSCHER

"Geologically speaking, Cape Cod is little more than a constantly shifting sand bar.
—BRIAN MORRIS, WCAI, LOCAL NPR STATION

Spring finds last year's fire road
winter-crumpled into the ocean.
On the radio,
the geology professor says:

we can have buildings or
we can have beaches; we cannot have both.

I walk to the cliff-edge—crane
over the ocean's bitemark,
to see the scar—
I measure, how much, how far,
but cannot fathom what is gone.

A flight of swallows swoops and dances
in the space that was sand.

I want it back:
yesterday, the fire road; I want
sunsets and seals; I want
wild lilies in the woods; I want
to walk along the precipice,
to balance on the edge
of earth and sea, now
and then; I want to hold—
in the cup of my mouth—
the sun and the moon and the summer
and my breath forever, but
the ocean has other plans.

*Protecting the seashore has left
a dynamic coastline*, the professor says.

I bring you to see: the scrub pine torn
from the edge, tossed into the sand
like a bone sucked clean of flesh,
a fishbone or a wishbone—snapped
between two hands—which one is lucky?

*In their natural state,
dunes and shorelines come and go.*

The professor says, the shoreline
is supposed to change, erode, evolve.

That very shoreline—the one that attracted us—
must vanish in order to exist.

We have two choices: he says,
let the water in or try to keep it out.

We are drawn to magenta cloud, jet sea;
moontide and riptide transform us,
reshape us. We cling to a shoreline
crumbling in our hands.

Learning to live with water,
                              there is a dawning,

Everything, everything is ephemeral—
everything closes, empties, evaporates.
Laughter fades into silence.
Light into darkness.
Even darkness, given time,
disappears.

About This Story

Long a desired destination for summer travelers and second home
buyers, Cape Cod is in the midst of a housing crisis. The COVID-19
pandemic drove the wealthy to buy homes outside cities while also
enabling more people to work remotely, pushing up the demand for
housing in places like the Cape. Consequently, the cost of the few
available homes has become astronomical, decreasing available
housing for year-round and lower-income cape residents. But this

poem by Adeline Carrie Koscher, who lives and writes on the Cape, reveals an existential problem that supersedes this man-made crisis.

The Cape has always been subject to wind and water, erosion and tides. What we love about this land is also the reason it was never suited for permanent dwellings, especially as climate change accelerates sea level rise and erosion of the shoreline. Seafarers have long picked up and moved their homes and stations, just as the tides have long carried the wrack of beaches to and fro along the cape's shorelines. The more one learns about the natural history and geology of this landscape, the more one questions attempts at permanence and the wisdom of settling here long term. Part of loving this place is learning to accept and live without what has drawn and connected people to it, as Koscher captures here and as Mary Oliver conveys in her poem "In Blackwater Woods": "To live in this world you must be able to do three things: to love what is mortal; to hold it against your bones knowing your own life depends on it; and, when the time comes to let it go, to let it go."

We discovered Koscher's poem in the 2021 collection *From the Farther Shore: Discovering Cape Cod and the Islands Through Poetry*, but it was previously published by WCAI and in *Canary: A Literary Journal of the Environmental Crisis*. Koscher explains that she crafts works of short fiction and poetry as a conduit for wonder, solace, and vitality, and that she aims to suffuse her writing with joy—even as she acknowledges her longing to get back what time and tides have carried away.

The Beach

CLARE LEIGHTON

Excerpt from *Where Land Meets Sea: The Tide Line of Cape Cod*

When we think of the beach on Cape Cod, we mean the vast expanse of the back shore—the back side, as they call it here—facing the Atlantic. The gentler side, nestled in the curve of the arm of the Cape, is never the beach; it is always the bay. And, though both are built of sand and both are subject to the rhythm of the tides, yet they are utterly different. Even the life upon their shores is different; horseshoe crabs and scallops, oysters and clams cannot be found along the Atlantic at low water; they require the shelter of the bay.

This, fringing the Atlantic, is an austere, wild world. Over a large part of the year it is a lonely world, visited only by the little animals and the birds. Deer can be seen here, and skunks, and the tern nests upon the ground. Deserted sands border an empty sea.

"I remember, just as far back as 1916, how there would be fifty to sixty vessels a day, out there on the back side, passing along on the horizon," says Charlie Mayo. "There was no Canal, then, to take them the other way. We used to see so many towboats and barges, all the year round. It's kind of forlorn today. I can scarcely stand going there, it's so lonesome."

But nobody could say that it is lonesome during the months of the summer. Looking at it then, with its golden sands and the smooth blue of the ocean—the sands dotted with bright, striped umbrellas and sun-tanned, happy swimmers looking upon this serene scene it is not easy to think of it as anything other than a mighty playground. Little family groups sit there, soaking up the sun, over the hours of daylight . . . .

"Let's go down to the beach," everyone says all summer long. But it is the visitors who say this. Not often do you see the real Cape Codders here. They know too much about this mighty mass of water and carry within them unwilling memories. Sometimes, after the summer people have left, they will go especially at the height of a storm. But they hold a strange proprietary respect for this Atlantic and are reluctant to share it with outsiders.

And it is little wonder that they feel this, for in their blood, and in the blood of their ancestors, lies tribute to the vagaries of this sea.

One day in late October I took a neighbor with me to watch a particularly wild tide. It was a high course tide, a forced one, urged upwards by a violent northeaster, so that it must have been, at the very least, fourteen feet. She was a gentle creature and recently widowed, and I feared lest she might not really want to go to the back shore in this fury of wind and rain. As we stood on the top of the dunes, watching the churning sea that undercut the cliffs and tossed the sand high into the air, I looked round at her, wondering what she was thinking and feeling.

"It's a mighty force, water is," she said quietly. "You can quench fire, but nothing on this earth can stop the force of water."

"I know something about it," she went on, her voice scarcely audible above the thump of the breakers. "My father was lost right out there. He was a sea captain."

A sense of shame covered me, and a feeling of humility. The woman grew suddenly ennobled before me as I thought of what was contained in those few words, so quietly spoken.

This made me think of the company of ghosts that must walk the beach, stepping with bewilderment around the sun bathers and the striped umbrellas.

There would be the earliest of the Indians, back in the unknown, the men whose bones have crumbled to become the sand itself. And then the Pilgrims, watching later tribes of Indians, peeping at them in apprehension and fear. The names of our beaches testify to this; First Encounter Beach, in Eastham, and Corn Hill, in Truro, where the Pilgrims were saved from starvation by finding a cache of Indian corn. These, walking their ghostly paths along the sand, might come across an occasional Dutch phantom, strayed from the early seventeenth-century trading post on Great Island. But most certainly they would meet the mighty company of the shipwrecked, ghosts tortured by the fury of the sea, frozen ghosts who had clung to the masts of sinking ships in the middle of winter, ghosts of mothers and children, sailing the high seas with their men. They might also meet the unhappy, haunted ghosts of wreckers who had plundered the grounded vessels. . . .

Walking this beach they would know, with the supersensitive awareness of the disembodied, exactly where the ribs of ships lay buried beneath the sand and comprehend the sudden appearance upon the surface of this sand of the vertebra of a whale, disclosed by the violence of a northeaster.

But most of all, I like to think, they would have felt fellowship with the men who used to walk the beach on the watch patrol, keeping them company upon their desolate dark journeys. . . .

But let us forget the past, for a little while, and enjoy the beach, walking along this ever-changing, lacy-edged tide line in the space between high-water mark and low. The tide line is fringed with sea wrack: golden seaweed, deep brown seaweed, long switches of seaweed, like the tufted tails of some unknown animals; little shells, broken shells, shells of many kinds; pebbles bright-colored from the water. But there is something else to be found along this tide line. Here lie the delicate filigrees of bleached fish bones, these white, Gothic-like, intricate patternings of such beauty. What fish do they come from? And how long did it take the sun and the salt water to bleach them to this purity? You question, and all you know is that they lie here, on the sand, some of the most exquisite of nature's designs.

Looking at them I find myself singing the verse of an old Cape Cod song:

> *Cape Cod girls*
> *They have no combs.*
> *They comb their hair*
> *With codfish bones.*

But with the normal acquisitiveness of those who walk the beach—that acquisitiveness which even a moralist like Thoreau was finding hard to resist—an acquisitiveness that would brand one as a thief, anywhere other than in that narrow strip of sand, between high tide and low, I, too, search upon the shore for what I can find. After a three-day northeaster I am as rapacious as anyone. I haul great logs and branches of beautiful silvered driftwood along the beach and pack them in the back of my car. (Once I brought an enormous root of a tree back with me, all the way from the tip of Cape Breton. But that was not for burning; it stands, now, on a Connecticut hillside in its smooth silver beauty, reminding me always of the far North.)

As the driftwood burns in the fireplace, tossing the strangest blues and greens into the yellow flames, it brings the magic of the unknown. This hunk of wood, satin-smooth and bleached by the ocean, stained brown in places from the rust of nails where did it come from? Was it part of a ship, wrecked up the coast? Or a tree, uprooted in a storm? Conjecture brings an element of romance to the fire burning in the grate.

But this element of romance is not all, for the essence of the beachcomber lies even deeper. It satisfies, I believe, the privileged lawlessness of mankind. The sand of the beach carries upon its surface objects tossed up by the sea, from hundreds of miles away, belonging to nobody on this earth. And why, then, should we not grab them? Sister at heart at all wreckers, I grab with the rest. . . .

So long as the tide line will give us shells we are all right. Then, in entire honesty, we can satisfy this crazy urge. For which of us has not collected shells? Early each year indiscriminatingly we start. And then, as the summer passes, we grow progressively selective, till the inevitable moment comes when we look at our greedy amassings and decide to toss them away. Out go the slightly imperfect scallop shells, the big whelk with a flaw, the little fairy boats in which we had so deeply delighted. And why do we do this? And what do we leave? A gap, and a need, awaiting fulfillment next year.

But we have few shells, up here on Cape Cod. I say this as I fling my mind back to the years I spent in the South. There, along the shores of the Carolinas, on those sands that are silver, rather than golden, you could not avoid treading upon shells, there were so many. The sand was covered with the fragile hinged tellens, colored like subtle rainbows. The beaches were blossoming sea meadows.

And then, traitor, still, to the Cape, I think of the little pools of Maine, where the water stays behind at low tide, imprisoned in the hollows of rocks. There, within the boundaries of a few rocks, you can see in microcosm the whole world of color and shapes.

But this treachery does not stay with me for long. I remember, suddenly, the great expanse of sand, upon the back shore, and the feeling of calm space. I see it at night, in the summer, at the height of a heat wave, with an orange moon rising over the sea and the offshore wind bringing a sickly sweet land-scent, a mixture of pines and sweet fern, that overpowers any scent from the sea. The tide is very low, and you can wade out towards the path of the moon that is bronzing the water, feeling, rather than perceiving, the edge of the ocean. You can wade across to the sand bars, and even the guzzles reach only up the thigh. It is a gentle, benign sea, on such a night. And I remember other nights, at the full of the moon, with the scattering flurry of sandpipers before me, as I walk the edge of the ocean. Again this ocean holds no hint of danger.

And I know that this beauty of gentle calmness is every bit as much a part of our back shore as are the furies of winter. So, too, is the summer sunrise over this sea, bursting upon the sand dunes in a splendor of sudden gold.

But I believe there is something else about the beach that comforts and delights us. More than pleasure in the beauty of sand—sand ribbed and patterned by the lapping and pounding of the water, sand covered with the tell-tale marks of the feet of the birds, or the flurry swept by the tips of their feathers; more even than pleasure in the ocean itself, there is the awareness of the rhythm of the tides.

For we have need of this rhythm. Watching the discipline of the tides, with their evident rhythm, we can surrender our fears, reminded that we are part of the universe and live within the pattern of an order that is beyond our control. The fisherman is aware of this. Working with the swing of the tides that he cannot avoid and is unable to ignore, he carries within him a deep, wise patience that nothing can destroy. From him we can learn.

About This Story

We first came across the work of Clare Leighton in the Sturgis Library in Barnstable, pulling her 1954 book *Where Land Meets Sea* from the shelves of the oldest building that houses a public library in America. This building, dating from 1644, was originally the home of the founder of Barnstable, Reverend John Lothrop, and is among the oldest houses remaining on Cape Cod. Leighton's book initially captivated us with the ornate nautical pattern on its cover, and we found ourselves thumbing through the pages in awe of her unique ability to capture the fury and beauty of this place through both words and engravings.

Born in London, Leighton traveled to America multiple times on lecture tours in the 1920s and 1930s following her studies at fine art schools. She ultimately decided to move to America in 1939, first settling in North Carolina, then moving to Woodbury, Connecticut, and finally planting herself in Wellfleet on Cape Cod, where she continued to write and create wood engravings that largely depicted pastoral life and various laborers. A magazine article entitled "The Industrious Artist: Clare Leighton," quotes her as saying, "Actually the artist is always working. By this I don't mean sitting at a desk engraving or at an easel painting. Probably the most important part of the work is when one is doing nothing but observing and tucking away into the unconscious those things perceived that seminally wait to be transformed into rhythms and designs."

Leighton's primary medium was woodblock engravings and prints. She created nearly nine hundred woodblocks in her lifetime, which she exhibited across the world and published in more than a dozen of her own books. But she also created works in glass, paint, ceramics, and words. Her musings and stories of her experiences on Cape Cod are just as detailed, timeless, and alluring as her etchings.

In the Presence of Shadows: A Meditation

ELIZABETH BRADFIELD

Before jumping into the ocean, which I do as often as I can on the Outer Cape, I stand, waves surging up over my knees, sand pulling out from under my heels, and stare.

I stare a long time, as wind pushes, as sounds roil, and gradually I assimilate a sense of the sea and suss the dangers: undertow? seals? frenzy of feeding birds? smooth sheen or fishy whiff? How many people (how alone am I)? How turbid and confusing is the water?

I am looking, of course, for sharks. Not sharks in general, but for a White Shark seeking a meal, waiting to lunge, mistaking me for something with more blubber.

When I first approached this place in the late 1990s as a washashore from the Salish Sea, I reveled in this mercurial ocean, which could be calm as the most protected harbor and did not stay invigoratingly cold all year, but in late summer allowed me to float easily, warm and gentle, then raged up into a frenzy of breakers as a front passed through.

Sharks were the furthest thing from my mind.

As a naturalist on the whale watch boats, I soon learned the thrill of seeing a basking shark's chocolate brown body and glowing white open mouth as she swam slowly, allowing plankton to flow in over sandpaper teeth and out through massive gills. I learned the mind-boggling indigo of blue sharks, the "blue dogs of August," which glow in the summer's green sea.

Once, just off Race Point, a splashing caught my eye. It was a calm, sunny day, and we'd been seeing schools of tuna, purple clouds of menhaden, huge flocks of shearwaters, humpback whales bubble-net feeding together. When the captain and I turned to look, even though I'd never seen one in my life, I knew instantly it was a thresher shark. Thresher sharks have a tail like the Grim Reaper's scythe, the top half almost as long as their body. The tail is used to stun small fish. *Thwack*, the long tail flexing in air, coming down hard. *Thwack*. I will never forget this moment.

It would be nearly twenty years before I'd see a White Shark.

The following shark species are allowed to be harvested in Massachusetts:

> *smooth dogfish, spiny dogfish, Atlantic sharpnose, bonnet-head, finetooth, blacknose, tiger, blacktip, spinner, bull, lemon, nurse, scalloped hammerhead, great hammerhead, smooth hammerhead, porbeagle, common thresher, oceanic whitetip, blue*

The following species are prohibited from harvest in Massachusetts:

> *silky, sandbar, sand tiger, bigeye sand tiger, whale, basking, white, dusky, bignose, Galapagos, night, Caribbean reef,*

narrowtooth, Caribbean sharpnose, smalltail, Atlantic angel,
longfin mako, shortfin mako, bigeye thresher, sharpnose
sevengill, bluntnose sixgill, bigeye sixgill

In spiny dogfish season, go down to the Chatham Pier and watch as box after box of fawn-dappled sharks about as long as your arm are offloaded for sale.

Commercial landings of spiny dogfish in Massachusetts totaled 3.8 million pounds in 2022. Most caught (81 percent) are female. Most are sent to England (fish and chips). I come upon their bodies sometimes when I walk the back shore, tossed out after someone setting nets for another species hauls them up and has to chuck them back. "Bycatch" is the term.

Female spiny dogfish live around thirty years and don't start reproducing until they are twelve, giving birth to litters of five to six "pups." They have one of the longest known gestation periods, up to two years. They hunt in packs of thousands. I wonder what their sensitive ampullae of Lorenzini—organs most sharks have that detect minuscule electrical currents created by the beings around them—sense in the midst of such company. They must be thrillingly, maybe even titillatingly, abuzz with presence.

The eyes of a spiny dogfish are a metallic hazel-flecked green, like an opal.

The Monster Shark Tournament (MST) is one of seventy shark-fishing tournaments held annually on the East Coast. The meat of tournament sharks is often donated to food banks; one year, more than thirty-four hundred pounds of steaks were donated. Tournament sharks are made available to biologists who, short on funding and time, appreciate any specimen they can get to study. Tournaments prefer "fighters" like blue, mako, thresher, and porbeagle sharks.

A couple of winters ago, I was walking out to Jeremy Point in Wellfleet and came upon a stranded porbeagle, gray, solid, thick, with the jagged teeth of legend. I lay down alongside him. He was longer than me. Most sharks in our waters migrate in and out, following their favored temperatures and prey, but the porbeagle, like me, is a year-rounder.

In Provincetown, there are two replicas of a shark hung for weighing: one at the entrance to a commercial parking lot, one between the public restrooms and the Portuguese Bakery.

> . . . *What is more built*
> *for winning than the swept-back teeth,*
> *water-finished fins, and pure bad eyes*
> *of these old, efficient forms of appetite . . .*
> —ALAN DUGAN, "PLAGUE OF DEAD SHARKS"

When we say "shark" here, though, most people think of great whites. The one from *Jaws*, a movie that many say has scarred them for life, scared them of the water. "Do you still swim?" ask visitors as they stare longingly at the beautiful, inviting ocean.

There were eleven shark-related fatalities worldwide in 2021. Every year there are more than one hundred drownings related to rip currents. Cape Cod lifeguards perform thirty rip current rescues per season at each of our four National Seashore surf beaches.

Living alongside apex predators is not unfamiliar to me. I worked as a naturalist in Southeast Alaska, as well as on Svalbard and on Baffin Island, for twenty-five years, work that included leading walks with one eye out for bears (polar or grizzly). When I lived for five years in Anchorage, my daily dog walks were in woods where bears walked, too.

What's that final line of Mary Oliver's poem? How, knowing she shares her walk with a bear, she feels that "every leaf on the whole mountain is aflutter."

White Sharks are returning to our waters thanks to both protection and opportunity. In 1997, White Sharks were federally designated a protected species; Massachusetts, in 2005, doubled down, prohibiting capture in state waters up to 3 miles out. Since the 1960s, when gray seals were protected in Massachusetts, these adaptable marine mammals have been recovering from their near extirpation. Each feeds the other.

I've never seen a White Shark from shore, not even in the hundreds of hours I've spent documenting and observing the sites where seals come to rest together, the place where literature and lore say White Sharks lurk. I've never seen one lunge up from where she's waiting, waiting, waiting for the right seal at the right time. I know it happens; I've heard stories and seen the wounds—old and healed or fresh pink—on seals who have narrowly escaped those jaws.

Every public beach on the Outer Cape now has a huge sign with a photo of a shark swimming toward the viewer, mouth open, gills scratched by seal claws. In the corner, there's a graph showing the relative abundance of White Sharks in our waters, month by month. Beside the sign, a "stop the bleed" kit. We are encouraged to download the Sharktivity App, and lifeguards get everyone *Out of the water!* when a shark is seen.

But I think about all the sharks out there we haven't seen, that aren't tagged. I think about the friend of a friend who dives for lobster. One day, he dropped off the side of his boat, got his mask settled, and looked down: a White Shark rested below him on the edge of the drop-off, hovering, waiting. I think that a lot of a shark's life is about quiet waiting, feeling the heartbeats pulse through the water, smelling what the currents waft, attending to the ocean.

> *Carcharodon carcharias. Six thousand*
> *pounds of muscle powering a hoop*
> *of butcher's knives . . .*
> —MARK HADDON, "GREAT WHITE"

The first time I saw a White Shark, I was out on Stellwagen Bank. We spotted the fin, slowed the engines, and the shark turned toward us and then cruised down the side of the boat, calm and inevitable as moonrise. At one point, she (?) rolled her wide body, stared up at us with one blue-black eye, then sank out of vision and comprehension. I think all two hundred of us were holding our breath as we craned over the rail.

Twice, I've seen White Sharks feasting on the bodies of whales. Once, close to Herring Cove, the carcass was quickly surrounded by a frenzied melee of amped-up boaters. Several White Sharks circled, bit, and sank back. For the sharks, it must have been altogether too much: the blubber-stink, the close presence of so many other sharks, the electrical zing of engines. I watched as the stern of a small boat dipped, pulled by a shark, then released, bobbed. I was glad to leave.

The most beautiful encounter I have ever had with a White Shark was a few years ago. The pier had been abuzz with rumors of a whale carcass offshore. We went searching and found the young humpback floating belly-up. The tide was streaming around the body, pulling oil into the sea in a long, shiny slick, and the air was peppered with storm petrels, fluttering, hovering, dipping their bills.

We were all quiet, looking at the whale, watching the petrels dance and feast. And yes, there were sharks. Shadows in the water that didn't so much rise into view as appear, circling the body. Blue dogs, then—unmistakable—a huge female White Shark. She slid up the whale's flank, mouth open, eyes rolled back. She bit down and the blubber wobbled and shook.

I knew that soon the whale would sink. Other scavengers would take over the good work of converting the massive bulk into other energies for other lives. The bones would be stripped bare, scattered, and rest on the sea floor, oily and rich, new habitat.

I could have stayed there all day, listening to small wavelets break on the whale's body, startling at the emergence of one shark, another, thinking about the life of the whale, all the lives clustered around this windfall. How glad I was that there were sharks in the waters able to take advantage of such a huge gift, to have that circle completed.

Shadow (Carcharodon carcharias)

ELIZABETH BRADFIELD

*Ampullae of Lorenzini are sense organs that allow sharks
and rays to detect electrical fields and pulses (like heartbeats) in the water.*

For you, shadow, the skin-holding sea flickers,
surges with light, scent, the pulsed charges of
bird-heart, cod-heart, seal-heart.

    I have envied and feared those for whom the spirit veil
    is thin, who sense what to me is wind, but
    for them is presence beyond birds.

Your eye, I read, shadow, is able to see in both darkness and day,
is not black but indigo, a dye that harmed so many
more in its enslaved making than your hungers ever have.

Only twice have I been certain some spirit
hovered near me. Once, the night I was married,
on a sleeping porch beside the bay where I still swim.

You hover in the trough at slack tide, in the shadow
between sand bars, listening, listening with your other
senses, your body a tuning fork thrummed by other bodies.

We woke in the night in that borrowed house
on the bed in the winterized porch, something
unhappy on the other side of the wall. Something....

The quiet of you. How, the one time I saw you
from the cliff's ragged field site, you emerged more
than rose into sight, shadow, becoming presence.

A sound, a chair scraped. Thrum of ire. I held
my love and, instinctive, hardened into a shield, every
part of me no. And it faded. We could not return to dream.

I've seen what you've missed more than witnessed the taking:
punched curve at the hip of a seal, pink-white and new
or furred-over scar. I've seen you slide up a dead whale's flank.

The friend whose house it was, unsurprised, told us
her mother had died there, her last years full of confused
pain. What did her spirit speak or seek?

I read that your body, unlike the bodies of whales,
of turtles, of tuna, lucky shadow, is not hurt
by the poisons (PCB, Mercury) we've sloughed into your ocean.

I felt myself shift into pity, then. Fear and fury
ebbed. With the senses I have, I can't sense much
of the worlds I live alongside, signaling over me.

Shadow, the tags that sound out your passage are nothing
but moments of presence, nothing of what pulls
you or what changes the skin you can shade at will.

I don't seek or fear you but I know you're there,
under the bay's bright scrim, your senses vaster
and older than anything this body or the gray folds
of my human mind, fired by strange sparks, can know.

About These Stories

Meeting Elizabeth Bradfield felt, in ways, like meeting a long-lost
cousin who turned out to be *really cool*. We were introduced by our
mutual publisher of our respective anthologies. Liz is one of the
editors of the fabulous *Cascadia Field Guide: Art, Ecology, Poetry*—and
also happens to be a writer. We met on a gray late fall day in Truro
and walked across town from the market to the beach, a welcome
change of pace (literally) for our many interviews. While thoughtfully
answering our questions about the Cape, Liz would pause to point
out interesting landmarks or get excited about wildlife she spotted
flying or passing by on the quiet neighborhood road leading us to
Cold Storage Beach. This bayside beach is named for the historic
storehouses that were used to keep fish cold in the early 1900s, and
remain today as private residences and vacation rentals.

As we strolled the beach, our conversation wove together insights
into natural history, marine science, queer culture, climate change,

and the local community. One of the things we admire most about Liz is her joy and encyclopedic knowledge about the marine ecosystem of Cape Cod, so we were delighted when she invited us to join her on a Dolphin Fleet whale watch, where she works, at the end of the week. We joined Liz on the observation deck of the ship as the researchers looked out for whales and logged their IDs (based on images of their flukes).

On what the captains and Liz agreed was an unusually calm October day, we were treated to visits from many families of whales around us: one a juvenile who introduced me to logging (floating and rolling like a log), another that demonstrated the spectacle of a whale pooping, and another entangled in some kind of line or rope. We called the hotline and waited anxiously, keeping tabs while the Center for Coastal Studies Marine Animal Entanglement Response team made their way from Provincetown to help. When she wasn't talking about whales, Liz exuberantly shared her love and knowledge of the region's seals, fish, birds, and yes, sharks. We were both enjoying ourselves immensely, and neither of us wanted to head back in, despite my seven-hour drive back to Philadelphia that night, but dusk forced our hand and we headed to shore. Liz, binoculars in hand, kept a hopeful eye out for sharks, studying the shadows of the water, until the very last moment.

We were thrilled when Liz agreed to write about sharks for the book, a piece that felt missing from the material we were finding in our research and most fitting for her wonder at the marine world.

Long Point Light

MARK DOTY

Long Point's apparitional
   this warm spring morning,
      the strand a blur of sandy light,

and the square white
   of the lighthouse—separated from us
      by the bay's ultramarine

as if it were nowhere
   we could ever go—gleams
      like a tower's ghost, hazing

into the rinsed blue of March,
   our last outpost in the huge
      indetermination of sea.

It seems cheerful enough,
   in the strengthening sunlight,
      fixed point accompanying our walk

along the shore. Sometimes I think
   it's the where-we-will-be,
      only not yet, like some visible outcropping

of the afterlife. In the dark
   its deeper invitations emerge:
      green witness at night's end,

flickering margin of horizon,
   marker of safety and limit.
      But limitless, the way it calls us,

and where it seems to want us
   to come And so I invite it
      into the poem, to speak,

and the lighthouse says:
   Here is the world you asked for,
      gorgeous and opportune,

here is nine o'clock, harbor-wide,
   and a glinting code: promise and warning.
      The morning's the size of heaven.

What will you do with it?

About This Story

Synonymous with coastal beaches, lighthouses are particularly iconic on Cape Cod due to its history of shipwrecks in the treacherous waters of the Outer Cape. Before the Cape Cod Canal was created in 1914, ships navigating the Massachusetts coast regularly succumbed to storms, shoals, and shifting sandbars—it's estimated that more than three thousand ships were lost along the coast from Provincetown to Chatham. With an average of two shipwrecks a month occurring during winter, wreckers and beachcombers came to rely on treasures from the sea, salvaging valuable cargo, equipment, and materials from the wrecked ships. Lighthouses were built to help prevent disasters at sea, and life-saving services were established to take a more proactive approach to ensuring survivors.

Long Point Light in Provincetown is the most remote lighthouse within Cape Cod National Seashore and can be reached only by boat or a grueling several-mile hike through loose sand. Like many of Cape Cod's lighthouses, it has needed to be moved due to erosion, and its light has been automated to now run on solar power, though it shines only for historic and cultural purposes and no longer as an aid to navigation. A predecessor of the US Coast Guard, the US Life-Saving Service, built manned watchtowers every 5 miles, with smaller halfway shelters in between. At night, crews would patrol the beaches and walk to meet each other at the halfway stations, where they'd exchange medallions as proof of their night patrol. The crew would regularly run rescue drills to practice using the life-saving apparatus of the time: a small cannon known as a Lyle gun would shoot a projectile to which a light rope was attached, over the mast of a stranded vessel, and then a breeches buoy (a lifebuoy with canvas breeches attached) would be suspended from the rope and shipwreck victims would be hauled to safety, using it like a zip line. Today, you can see a reenactment in summer months at the Old Harbor Life-Saving Station at Race Point Beach.

Mark Doty moved to Provincetown with his then-partner Wally Roberts after Wally tested positive for AIDS in the late 1980s. They sought refuge and comfort in Provincetown's gay community as Wally became increasingly ill and ultimately passed in 1994. Doty's 1993 poetry collection *My Alexandria*—centered around the themes of mortality and life, beauty and loss, in the time of the AIDS/HIV crisis—received the National Book Critics Circle Award, the Los Angeles Times Book Prize, and the T. S. Eliot Prize. Doty subsequently stayed on in Provincetown for another ten years with his new (now former) partner Paul Lisicky—a novelist and memoirist who also wrote about Provincetown in the 1990s in his 2020 book *Later: My Life at the Edge of the World*.

Leaving Nauset Light

CASS DAUBENSPECK

We drive the flat, wild two-lane Route 6 to the Outer Cape twice a year: east from Pennsylvania toward Provincetown to the rotary in Orleans, the Salt Pond Visitor Center, Coast Guard Beach, and then to the crest of the dunes and Nauset Light. The landscape is dotted with pitch pines, bayberry, scrub grass, all so free and uninhibited, like the feeling rising in the backs of our throats as we suspect we've made it to the end of this eight-hour journey. And then that familiar red-and-white tower sitting up slightly above the road, spinning her rotating aerobeacons, letting us know for sure.

Nauset Light, one of fourteen lighthouses left on Cape Cod, gathers tourists every single day of the year. Even during a gale storm with winds at 45 mph, we watch through the little porch window as people tread up in their contorted windbreakers to stand in front of the lighthouse and take a selfie. Sometimes wearing a gnome hat, or with their best friend. Sometimes in a motorized wheelchair, or with several family members. Often holding a bag of potato chips with the picture of the lighthouse on it. On Thanksgiving Day, as we move some patio chairs out into the windy November afternoon, visitors come walking up the path to stand beneath the aerobeacons and take a picture.

Two teenage girls come within ten feet of us, giggling on the other side of the pine trees, wearing their pajamas. They don't see us, we don't think, until the dog barks.

I've been visiting the Nauset Lighthouse and staying in its keeper's cottage in Eastham, Massachusetts, since I was three years old. The golden yarrow, blue eryngium, and orange milkweed that grow all along the front garden beneath the porch were planted intentionally for their hardy temperament and complementary colors. A shade and privacy garden to the north of the house offsets a thicket of wild rugosa that spills everywhere over and beyond a short wall of wooden fencing facing west, the tenacious mauve blooms coming back every year to prove their toughness in the face of harsh coastal weather. An old picture shows my family on the porch of the keeper's cottage with Nauset Lighthouse reflected in the porch window, all of us squinting against the day's peak sun.

On this balmy November morning, the tide is low and the beach is strewn with trash and treasures from long distances—lobster traps, driftwood, dead trees. Every year, for many years, the stairs to Nauset Beach have been rebuilt and then gone, eaten by the tide. A winding pathway set way back from the dunes serves the public now as a trail to the ocean. Two years in a row, seal carcasses have been decomposing on the beach, covered with dried kelp, seagulls pecking at the reeking flesh. This isn't quite the Cape Cod I knew as a child. Tiny chickadees and towhees search the sandy paths around the residential dead-end zone on Nauset Light Beach Road, where cars once freely traveled. There's no denying it: Eastham is eroding. A chain gate tied up between two posts says "No Trespassing, Residents Only." The only driveway that remains beyond this barrier is for the keeper's house.

Down over the dunes you can see the remnants of homes that have been dismantled and lost to a receding coastline. I remember the small houses that lined the cliff, that were there when I was a little girl. Now, pipes and cords stick out of the side of the dune, a perilous disruption of the landscape.

Bundled in our big puffy coats, my husband and I, on a rare walk without the kids, watch quirky little wrens and yellow-breasted chats poke at insects on the blanched arms of the scrub oaks, unfazed by the cliff edge with its precarious overhang. We pick up sassafras leaves and trace their veins with our gloved hands, then stuff them into our pockets to add to our leaf collection. The white gulls fly in masses over the ocean, circling again and again, fishing until they tire. Looking out across the expanse—the bobbing seals riding the icy waves.

We return from our walk and warm up in the toasty house. We are here to commemorate what will be our last visit to the Nauset Lighthouse as owners of the keeper's cottage. In the spring, the keys will be handed over to the Nauset Light Preservation Society, which will manage the historical property without us. This was the deal.

My Aunt Mary first acquired the property in 1981—dragging my grandparents out to see it one day, following a phone call to the number in the real estate ad in the *New York Times*. I imagine them in my granddad's shiny brown Toyota Corona, tooling along the craggy road past Nauset High School, my grandmother Eleanor peering attentively out the window. Hundreds of feet separated "her" lighthouse from the sea, which gives you an idea of the intensity of erosion in Eastham. The most accurate estimation has been twelve to fifteen feet per year for the last few decades.

By 1996, when the distance between the cottage and the sea had become dangerous, Mary was encouraged to sell or move the cottage to another property. Voices from the outside said "cut and run." Certainly, dozens of homeowners on the Outer Cape had done just that, gone by the time Nauset had such worrisome proximity to the waves. But Mary couldn't. The tower had helped guide her through her own uncharted waters; it became her primary home during a difficult divorce, and then it became much more to so many of us, her brothers and nieces and nephews and grandnieces and grandnephews. I think she knew that, she had a feeling of it, and it was too much for her to *just cash out.*

Mary did not own the light tower itself, only the cottage and the oil house. Nauset Lighthouse was in the care of the Coast Guard, as are most lighthouses across America, at least those that are still active. According to Mary's notes, the Guard first published an official notice to mariners in September 1993 asking for feedback as they began to contemplate the future of the light. *Should they keep the lighthouse running? Or decommission it?*

Townspeople of Eastham took an interest in this question. Dismantling it was unacceptable. Nauset Lighthouse had put Eastham on the map. They wrote letters and editorials in local papers about keeping this local landmark intact and active. They were assured that their voices—not just the responses from mariners—would be taken into account. A few locals offered land that the lighthouse, the keeper's cottage, and the oil house could be moved to. And since the Coast Guard, underfunded for such efforts, was relinquishing control of the Nauset Lighthouse, the Nauset Light Preservation Society was formed. That grassroots effort has since been the support system for the light station and will take over the keeper's cottage when our family's tenure ends.

Mary made a very good and difficult decision when she decided to keep the house with its tower, even though it meant waging a multiyear battle with the National Seashore for permission to enter into a twenty-five-year lease ending in forfeiture, and then commencing a two-year project to hire house-moving expertise and equipment at her own personal and significant expense. She could have done an easier thing—moved the house to a different acreage, securing a different future for the building and letting all but the most investigative forget it had ever been part of the light station at all.

After the house was moved and Mary was much poorer, she now had a two-and-change-decades time frame to enjoy it before ultimately losing ownership when the lease was up. It's as though she knew, and we all know, it was not meant to be owned in the first place, but to be loved and shared by many. And now that would be its future.

When I think back on how my Aunt Mary must have felt, faced with the decision of what to do with her historical house, I think she never wavered in her belief that her role was that of a conservator. As an active community member in Eastham, she had a responsibility to fulfill. The people of Eastham recognize the inherently fragile nature of the woodlands and marshes behind the dunes, and they know that the best of intentions can ruin a place forever, change it irrevocably. Mary wanted to keep history from falling apart against the pressures of time and money, and because she could, she did. Especially in a time when all buildings are not created equal, we need to protect the ones that carry our oldest stories. The Nauset Light Station and each of its buildings, some of the last remaining antiquities of a disappearing coastal landscape, have safeguarded its chronicles since 1838, when lightkeeper Isaac Dunham first climbed out the scuttle door, presumably humming a choir song while scanning the sea for any sign of an off-course sailor.

Because of Mary's generosity, we are still here today, at the final end of the lease, looking out that window at the tourists taking photos, drinking our coffee on the porch just twenty feet from the tower. To give you a visual: at Nauset Light the buildings are arranged in a triangle on the wild piece of land delineated by Cable Road on the north and east sides, and Nauset Light Beach Road to the south. A bird's-eye map shows the light tower on the outermost corner, at the top of the hill, closest to the ocean. To its left is the oil house, where kerosene was kept as the light's energy source but is now mostly storage space for the Nauset Light Preservation Society. And in the third corner is the cottage, its red roof and worn cedar siding growing more handsome with age. The house makes the site feel complete, and strangers who come to see the tower feel naturally drawn over to it. One summer, when I was in the middle of a friendly conversation with a tourist, a man began to stomp past me up the stairs to the front porch, headed for the front door. Startled, I offered that the place was actually not a museum but a private residence. "I thought it was open to the public," he said, apologizing. Not yet, I said.

My son, Roman, sits up on his blue highchair in the sunlit kitchen eating eggs, dropping every other handful or so to the floor for the dog. My daughter lies on her back on the windowsill cushion, looking up into the blue pine tree that sits just outside of it, offering privacy from tourists and subtle shade in a particularly sunny portion of the main sitting room. She hums to herself as she stares up into its branches, listening to the dull crash of the ocean waves in the distance. Her mouth moves, talking to some unknown friend. I watch her and know that as a five-year-old I did exactly what she is doing, in that exact spot. There is so much of that happening lately—me watching my children in this house and remembering myself as them, memories running through my mind, colliding with their realities. I see them running around the base of the lighthouse playing hide-and-seek, remembering how I could run around and around forever, always just beyond my brother's reach.

I stand at the wood block counter, chopping celery, and imagine it is 1981. My Aunt Mary, having just acquired the place, humbly decorates, sands the floors with a friend, paints the walls with a brother, generally keeps the same vein of decor as its previous owner, Miriam Rowell, someone she deeply admired. Nothing has really changed in this house since then—the pantry, the bead-board walls, the enamel "Salle De Bain" sign on the downstairs lavatory, the map of Cape Cod shipwrecks hanging upstairs in the lemon-yellow guest room. I imagine Mary cooking supper, standing right here where I am, washing her hands in this sink and wiping them on her corduroys. I can almost hear her laugh, then add some witty quip to the joke in her low, warm voice.

In writing this I become aware of my own flawed propensity to become attached to physical things—places, objects, houses, people—that are nevertheless threatening to change, to leave us, to fall into the sea. When Mary died of cancer in 2001, it felt like a loss so deep, even my fourteen-year-old self understood and never has recovered from its magnitude. I am attached to Nauset Light, despite its never having "belonged" to me. And losing it this year feels like losing Mary all over again.

In my forty years of knowing it well, the lighthouse has taught me more about change than constancy, about detachment, perhaps, as much as devotion. And about the necessity of guides, of concrete touchpoints, to help us on our path, to keep us from going too far off course in this life. Mary was the kind of person who makes a strong impression and never leaves you the same. She believed in big moves, she was stalwart, and she left that legacy behind her of people who will tread through murk for what they believe in. Eventually the sun shines, even if feebly.

The future of the keeper's cottage will soon be in the hands of the people who helped Mary when she needed it, who supported her efforts and her belief that the buildings should stay together. I stare into the tide, watch it lap away at the sand, see the vibrant stones rolling and chafing and clattering together as the waves recede. In the end, I think it is not where we live or where we are but how we finally leave a place that matters.

About This Story

We visited the Nauset Light on an overcast day in late October, catching the last volunteer-led lighthouse tour of the season and an opportunity to climb the spiral staircase to peer out over the Atlantic from the lookout room. Its tight quarters limit volunteers to sending small groups ten at a time, and in these days of intense selfie culture and the insatiable urge to take *pics or it didn't happen*, this meant waiting our turn as many visitors directed their Insta-worthy shots. As we were waiting in line, we realized why this lighthouse felt so familiar—not only because we had visited on a brief trip years ago on a similarly dreary winter day but also as it was perhaps the most iconic lighthouse in New England.

The lighthouse is famous not for its bold red-and-white paint job or any particular footnote in the history books, but for its prominence on . . . a potato chip bag. Yes, the Nauset Light is *the* lighthouse that's featured on each bag of Cape Cod Kettle Cooked Potato Chips. Having inherited my dad's disposition for people watching, I looked on as groups of family and friends strolled over from the parking lot, potato chip bags in hand, eyes and smiles lighting up as they craned their heads to take in the structure that adorned their single-serve snack bags. I hadn't put it all together until I was offered an unopened bag of chips that had served merely as a prop for a family portrait. I could not sort out if I was amused or enraged by our very odd and peculiar species.

To distract myself, I attuned my ears to a conversation between a Nauset Light Preservation Society volunteer and a visitor who was inquiring about the house in front of us. The volunteer explained that it was the keeper's house and though it was historically and currently a private residence, the terms of the private lease would expire in 2023—twenty-five years after it was moved due to erosion and ownership changing hands. I recall wondering about the family living in this house who had "kept" the lighthouse all this time—what it must be like to open your doors and windows not to the serenity of the dunes or the roar of the ocean but to selfie-snapping tourists scattered about your front yard, potato chip bags in hand. Just a month later, I received an email from Cass Daubenspeck, who wanted to write about the family who lived in the keeper's house— *her own*. Cass teaches writing and literature, and ever since growing up at the Nauset Light, she's been interested in the cultural and historical significance of the Outer Cape region and how historical sites like the Nauset Light can contribute to the public's understanding and appreciation of the area's natural surroundings.

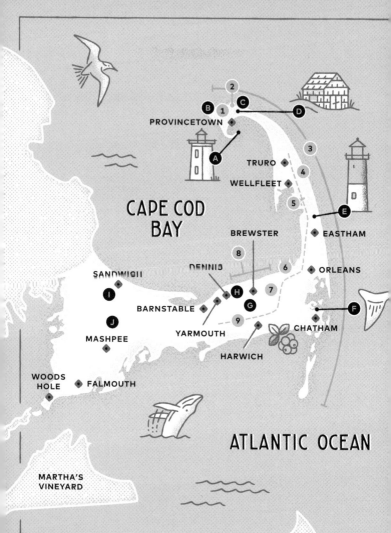

CAPE COD BAY

PROVINCETOWN

TRURO

WELLFLEET

BREWSTER

SANDWICH

DENNIS

BARNSTABLE

YARMOUTH

MASHPEE

HARWICH

WOODS HOLE

FALMOUTH

EASTHAM

ORLEANS

CHATHAM

ATLANTIC OCEAN

MARTHA'S VINEYARD

NANTUCKET ISLAND

N
W   E
S

EXPLORE

CAPE COD

✦

A guide for your next Cape Cod
adventure—on foot, by boat,
and by bicycle.

ATTRACTIONS

- **A** Long Point Light
- **B** Race Point Light
- **C** Old Harbor Life-Saving Station
- **D** Dune Shacks of Peaked Hill Bars Historic District
- **E** Nauset Light
- **F** Atlantic White Shark Conservancy Center
- **G** Cranberry Bog Tours
- **H** Cape Cod Museum of Natural History
- **I** Heritage Museum and Gardens
- **J** Mashpee Wampanoag Tribe Museum

NATURAL LANDMARKS

- **1** Blackwater Pond
- **2** Race Point Beach
- **3** Cape Cod National Seashore
- **4** Pamet Cranberry Bog Trail
- **5** Mass Audubon Wellfleet Bay Wildlife Sanctuary
- **6** Skaket Beach
- **7** Nickerson State Park
- **8** Brewster Flats
- **9** Cape Cod Rail Trail

What to Do

See the whales, by boat or from the shore.

No visit to Cape Cod is complete without whale watching. Situated along migration routes of several whale species and jutting out into nutrient-rich ocean where cold water currents and the warm Gulf Stream waters meet, Cape Cod is a *spectacular* place for viewing whales. The abundance of fish nearly guarantees multiple whale sightings, often of many whale species, depending on the season. One of our favorite Cape Cod memories was boarding a sunset whale watch at the end of a hot July day where we witnessed multiple mother and baby whales breaching, an exhilarating experience that left us speechless.

Hop aboard the **Dolphin Fleet Whale Watch** from Provincetown or **Hyannis Whale Watcher Cruises** in Barnstable. Whales can also be viewed from shore. Set your beach chair at **Race Point Beach** at the Cape Cod National Seashore in Provincetown or look down and out from the top of the dunes at **Longnook Beach** in Truro. Keep your eyes on the expansive panorama of the Atlantic Ocean, where you will likely also spot seals.

Bike the Cape Cod Rail Trail.

The **Cape Cod Rail Trail** is a paved, well-marked, and relatively flat bike trail that runs for more than 25 miles from South Dennis to South Wellfleet, passing through several towns, including Dennis, Harwich, Brewster, Orleans, and Eastham. Built on the right-of-way of an old railroad that transported freight and people for a hundred years, the trail is among the most scenic ways to experience Cape Cod. It takes you to many points of interest, including the **Salt Pond Visitor Center** and the **Nauset Light** in Eastham, **Nickerson State Park** in Brewster, **Cranberry Bog Tours** in Harwich, all the way up to **Cape Cod National Seashore** in Provincetown—and you can even connect to the **Old Colony Rail Trail**, which takes you to Chatham. Bike rentals are available at the many bike shops, hotels, and motels along the trail, and the towns en route offer a selection of restaurants to quench your hunger and thirst.

Stroll the narrow streets of Provincetown.

It's no wonder this is a place that people return to year after year. **Provincetown** is a vibrant and unique town, surrounded by stunning natural beauty that is worthy of a visit when traveling to Cape Cod. The cultural mecca of the Cape, P-town has no shortage of restaurants, bars, museums, charming shops, and entertainment. The town is a haven for artists, writers, and the LGBTQ+ community—a place where all are welcome and accepted as they are. Ditch your car and travel into the heart of town by foot or bike, as these narrow streets are difficult to find parking on and are better meandered through. Provincetown can be extremely crowded during peak season with tourists and summer residents, so if this isn't your scene, consider visiting during shoulder seasons in spring, early summer, or fall.

Paddle or stroll around saltwater marshes and ponds.

While best known for its more than 500 miles of sandy shoreline, Cape Cod has so much more to offer than just the ocean that surrounds it. The biodiversity of Cape Cod's many marshes and ponds make them a must for exploration on foot or by kayak. Be sure to visit Mary Oliver's muse, **Blackwater Pond**, by way of a relatively flat and easy trail in the Cape Cod National Seashore. One of our favorite stops was the **Wellfleet Bay Wildlife Sanctuary**, which offers an absolutely stunning array of ecosystems to explore, including a salt marsh, a sandy barrier beach, and pine woodlands. This sanctuary also provides the All Persons Trail—a self-guided, fully accessible nature trail so everyone can experience the very special nature of Wellfleet Bay.

If you want to get out on the water, several outfitters across Cape Cod offer kayak rentals and tours. This is a fantastic way to access pristine tucked-away tidal marshes where shorebirds, osprey, egrets, and herons gather, and where you can peer down through clear, calm bay waters to see clams, crabs, and fish—or find yourself in the midst of seals.

Hike through a wild cranberry bog to the ocean.

For a taste of one of the cape's most important crops and industries, head out to **Cranberry Bog Tours** in Harwich; **Cape Cod Cranberry Bog Tours** in East Sandwich, West Barnstable, or Chatham; or

Annie's Crannies in Dennis. Tours run seasonally and offer a glimpse into the operation of a cranberry bog, as well as the history and cultivation of this iconic crop that thrives in wet, temperate landscapes.

If you're looking for something more natural or self-paced, you can hike the **Pamet Cranberry Bog Trail** near Truro, through a former commercial cranberry bog that has been reclaimed by the wild and offers spectacular views of the Atlantic and the Pamet River valley, historic markers, and interpretive signage. Along the way, visit the old Pamet Cranberry Bog House and be sure to take the path over the dunes to the ocean. If you're visiting in the fall—harvest season—look below you for the distinctive red cranberries along the edges of the trail.

Short on time? Visit **Cape Cod Cranberry Harvest** in Harwich for homemade jellies to enjoy the spoils of the land.

Savor the local flavors.

Once so abundant with cod that you could easily catch them with a basket, Cape Cod is known for its seafood. Cod populations have declined, but lobster, clams, bay scallops, and Wellfleet oysters are plentiful. Try the clam chowder, grilled fish, and oysters at **Mac's Fish House** in Provincetown or **Mac's Shack** in Wellfleet. While lobster rolls are fresh and delicious from just about any restaurant on the Cape, if you're in a hurry **The Knack** in Orleans is a fast casual spot with spot-on lobster rolls—and that's coming from a lobster roll snob! Seafood not your thing? If you're in Provincetown, stop by local staples like **Liz's Cafe** for brunch perfection or **Spiritus Pizza** for a quick slice, or get a taste of local cuisine at **Jimmy's Hideaway**, where you'll need a reservation or can hang at the bar with the locals.

Beyond helping to build the various industries and communities across the Cape, Portuguese immigrants have left their mark on local cuisine. Be sure to taste your way through the Portuguese-inspired dishes when you see them on the menu or sample any dishes across the Cape featuring the signature linguiça, a Portuguese sausage. Stop by the **Provincetown Portuguese Bakery**, built in 1900 to feed hungry fishermen, for traditional Portuguese pastries. At **Salty Market** in Truro, try the egg and cheese breakfast sandwich on a homemade biscuit with linguiça added—trust us, *best sandwich ever*.

Take in museums, literature, history, and art.

Artists and writers have long found Cape Cod to be their place of inspiration. Dune shacks made from scraps of shipwrecks, mentioned by Henry David Thoreau in *Cape Cod*, used to serve as life-saving stations and later housed artists and writers like Jackson Pollock, Jack Kerouac, Tennessee Williams, and E. E. Cummings, who sought the silence and solace of these off-the-grid shacks. To see them for yourself, check out the **Peaked Hill Bars Historic District** and the **Dune Shack Trail**—or, to *really* experience them, apply for a week-long artist or writing residency.

Be sure to check the public programs calendar for events and talks at the **Fine Arts Work Center**, an internationally acclaimed collection of buildings and programs founded in 1968 by the likes of Stanley Kunitz that supports emerging writers and artists with fellowships, workshops, and residencies. Fellows have gone on to win the Pulitzer Prize, the National Book Award, and the MacArthur Fellowship, and have shown their work at the Venice Biennale, the Museum of Modern Art, the Whitney, and many other venues around the world. On the Upper Cape, take in history and art at the **Sandwich Glass Museum**—a standout museum dedicated to the art and industry of glass-making in the US.

To take home works that were inspired by or written in Cape Cod, stop by **Tim's Used Books** for a well-loved volume or swing by one of the many bookstores along the **Cape and Islands Bookstore Trail**, including some of our favorites: **Titcomb's Bookshop** in Sandwich, **Brewster Book Store** in Brewster, **Sea Howl Bookshop** in Orleans, and **East End Books** in P-town. Stop at the **Edward Gorey House** for a glimpse into the life and works of this renowned artist, or sample the many art galleries to see works from contemporary artists in towns like Wellfleet, Orleans, and Provincetown.

For history lovers, visit the charming **Provincetown Museum**, where you can find permanent and rotating exhibits on early and contemporary history, and climb to the top of the towering 252-foot **Pilgrim Monument**. Stop by the **Provincetown Public Library** and observe the half-scale replica of the schooner *Rose Dorothea* among the stacks of books on the second floor pointing toward the Cape Cod Room, where we did a lot of our research for this book. For a bit of maritime history, visit the **Old Harbor Life-Saving Station** at Race Point Beach in Provincetown, where you can catch reenactments of beach apparatus drills weekly through the summer and even go on an evening lantern tour led by the National Park Service on select dates through the fall. While in town, be sure to take in a drag or comedy show at the many venues along Commercial Street.

To learn more about Cape Cod's natural environment, visit the **Cape Cod Museum of Natural History**, which sits on more than 400 acres of land in Brewster and features exhibits on both the natural and cultural history of the region.

Visit the Cape's many lighthouses.

Perhaps you've seen some of the region's most iconic lighthouses—like the **Highland Light**, the **Nobska Point Light**, and the **Chatham Light**—depicted in paintings, or on a potato chip bag like the **Nauset Light**. These lighthouses stand handsomely any day, but be sure to check tour schedules online so you can peer *inside* them, too. Some lighthouses are accessible only by foot, boat, or four-wheeler, including the **Race Point Light**, the **Long Point Light**, and the **Wood End Light**. While the mileage of these popular hikes don't seem long, keep in mind that they can be strenuous as you're traveling long, sun-exposed stretches of loose sand. Before you set out, be mindful of the season, weather, and tides—and be sure to pack sunscreen and bug spray.

Learn about the Indigenous people of the Cape.

Visit the **Mashpee Wampanoag Tribe Museum** in Mashpee to learn about the history, culture, and traditions of the Wampanoag, who have lived on Cape Cod for thousands of years. A permanent exhibit, *Our Story: The Complicated Relationship of the Indigenous Wampanoag and the Mayflower Pilgrims,* created in collaboration with a Wampanoag creative agency, can be viewed at the **Pilgrim Monument and Provincetown Museum**. The *People of the Land: The Wampanoag* exhibit at the **Cape Cod Museum of Natural History** was created in partnership with the Plimoth Patuxet Museums (formerly Plimoth Plantation) and modern-day Wampanoag and features artifacts that show how Native people lived on this land.

Stroll through the **Heritage Museums and Gardens** in Sandwich to go inside a wetu, a traditional Wampanoag home, as well as visit the various rotating interpretive exhibits. When not rescuing land, the **Native Land Conservancy** offers a multitude of cultural preservation events and programs, such as hikes, cleanups, and opportunities for tribal members to participate in cultural workshops and wetu construction projects. Pick up copies of books written by Wampanoag authors, such as *Keepunumuk: Weeâchumun's Thanksgiving Story* and *Colonization and the Wampanoag Story*.

Have a beach day, every day.

Yes, we know—you didn't need a guidebook to tell you to *go to a beach* when visiting Cape Cod. Given its more than 500 miles of shoreline, the Cape offers a plethora of beach options, so we wanted to highlight some considerations for choosing which to visit. **Bayside beaches** along the north edge of Cape Cod offer calmer water and winds, slightly warmer water temperatures, and stunning sunsets; features like tidal flats, marshes, kettle ponds, sandbars, and tide pools; and very generous low tides that allow families with young kids to play safely for long stretches in shallow waters.

Ocean-side beaches are more exposed to the extremes of the Atlantic Ocean, so here you'll find more powerful waves, dynamic winds and weather, and dramatic dunes that  protect the areas inland. These beaches are especially beloved by surfers and boogie boarders, and those who like to feel the pull of the ocean. All beaches are rich with wildlife, including seals and sharks, so it is very important to be shark smart and swim at beaches with lifeguards. Beaches can be extremely crowded in warm months, with parking lots often filled by early morning, so consider visiting during off-seasons like spring and fall to enjoy the beautiful coastlines without the crowds.

Get your fill of marine science and research.

The **Atlantic White Shark Conservancy** has two locations, in Chatham and Provincetown, each offering different exhibits designed to educate and engage families with white shark research, conservation, and natural history. It also offers excursions with naturalists as they conduct shark research, checking receiver buoys that detect sharks and track data out on the water, as well as private white shark charters to see them in the wild. The **Center for Coastal Studies (CCS)** in Provincetown, dedicated to understanding, preserving, and protecting marine ecosystems and the coastal environment, offers many programs and events for the public, so be sure to check their calendar when planning your visit.

The **Woods Hole Oceanographic Institution** in Woods Hole is a mecca for marine research and home to the world's largest community of ocean scientists and engineers. Here you can visit the **Woods Hole Science Aquarium**, the country's oldest public aquarium, and the **statue of Rachel Carson** at Waterfront Park that commemorates the time she spent in Woods Hole, which influenced her books *Under the Sea-Wind, The Sea Around Us,* and *The Edge of the Sea.* You can explore the historic seaside village campus by taking a walking tour, stopping in at the **Ocean Science Discovery Center**, and browsing the **WHOI Store**.

Stroll the sand flats at low tide.

When the day is closing, make your way to a bayside beach and slip under the spell of a Cape Cod sunset. An insider tip from a local sent us to the **Brewster Tidal Flats**, which you can access from any public beach in Brewster. It's especially magical if low tide coincides with sunset, as it did for us. Here you can walk along the sand flats that stretch out for miles and reflect the prism of warm colors swirling above and below you—there's nothing quite like it. We suggest **Skaket Beach** in Orleans, just north of Brewster.

How to Visit Well

Leave no trace.

Cape Cod sees four to five million visitors each year, a majority of whom converge in the warm summer months—a high volume of foot traffic for a narrow stretch of land already exposed to extreme winds, waves, and weather from the Atlantic Ocean. This makes it all the more important for visitors to treat this landscape with care and recreate responsibly. Leave the natural environment as you found it, pack out trash and dispose properly, drive only on designated beaches, park only in designated areas, protect shorebird nests by following pet regulations on trails and beaches, don't feed the foxes or other wildlife, and stay on trails to protect fragile ecosystems.

Support nonprofits and land trusts.

With the Cape Cod National Seashore protecting only 41 miles of Cape Cod's shoreline, local land trusts and nonprofits play a significant role in protecting Cape Cod from increasing development. The Compact of Cape Cod Conservation Trusts supports thirty-one regional land trusts and watershed associations by providing technical expertise to preserve critical lands that provide walking trails and protect the public water supply, scenic views, wildlife habitat, and

Cape Cod's character. This includes organizations like Barnstable Land Trust, which offers educational programs and events for the public year-round, and Native Land Conservancy, a Native-led land conservation org that rescues land from development and degradation, in addition to preserving the traditional cultural lifeways that Indigenous people have practiced in their ancestral homelands for thousands of years.

If you've enjoyed land conserved by one of these local nonprofits—whether you've benefited from a natural viewshed by taking pictures of pristine landscapes or found connection and comfort in the quiet and solace of the woods—consider donating to these organizations to share your gratitude and help them continue their work.

Be shark smart.

The waters of Cape Cod are seeing a resurgence of the native Atlantic white shark population, thanks to the rebounding of seal populations after seals—a significant food source for sharks—were hunted to near extinction. While it's encouraging to see the return of a healthy and wild marine ecosystem, it means that white sharks are numerous along beaches where seals swim close to shore and where human residents swim and surf. All beaches in Cape Cod are adorned with purple flags with a white shark silhouette to remind visitors of their presence in the ocean—and many beaches are equipped with bleeding kits, which include military-grade equipment like tourniquets and bandages with a coagulant to help stop bleeding.

Cape Cod residents and visitors, many of whom have witnessed this increase in the shark population in their lifetime, have needed to adapt to new safety guidelines. Being shark smart includes being aware that sharks hunt in shallow waters and not swimming in areas where seals and schools of fish are visible, as well as water that is murky or with low visibility. Swimmers, paddlers, and surfers should always avoid isolating themselves by staying in groups. They should avoid splashing and stay close to shore where lifeguards can see them and rescuers can reach them. By being shark smart, we can continue to celebrate the sharks' return and model how we can coexist.

Consider where you stay.

Development is booming on Cape Cod, and many residential properties sit vacant much of the year because they're owned by seasonal residents or they're strictly rental properties—driving up housing prices and limiting the housing inventory for those who are or aspire to be full-time residents. While the issue is complex, there are things visitors can do to support full-time local residents and the local economy. Staying at locally owned hotels, motels, inns, and B&Bs, as opposed to chains, is a great way to support local economies. Many of these motels and inns have been updated to feel more modern, offer keyless and check-in-free accommodations, and even provide amenities like bikes or beach chairs and toys.

If you are booking through online vacation rental services like Airbnb or VRBO, look to see if your prospective host is a full-time resident. If so, perhaps your stay in their guest bedroom or guesthouse is funding their ability to live on Cape Cod year-round as artists or writers or people piecing together a patchwork of part-time and low-paying jobs. You can also read their listing or bio to see what they are doing to support the community and environment around them—like maintaining a natural pesticide-free garden instead of a green lawn, or offering composting for guests.

Buy local.

Purchasing goods produced by Cape Codders is a fun way to support the local economy *and* get a feel for the authentic Cape Cod. It's easy to do here as Cape Cod is brimming with artists, writers, farmers, and fishermen, and has many small towns lined with local businesses and boutiques, including Chatham, Falmouth, Harwich, Orleans, Provincetown, and Wellfleet—all of which also have lively and bountiful farmers markets throughout summer and into October. Buy direct from local producers or visit one of the many local shops, markets, and restaurants that carry their wares, harvests, and day's catch. This way you're supporting local families and their livelihoods, and preserving the local culture and community that make this a special place. Not only are you keeping money within the community and encouraging sustainable practices, but you are also lessening your carbon footprint by saving the energy inherent in transportation and shipping.

Towns to Visit

Brewster is known for historic sea captain homes. Here you will find quintessential Cape Cod–style homes and architecture along serene landscapes, from ponds to shorelines. Browse its charming shops and antique stores, including the Brewster Store, a historic general store with knickknacks, penny candy, jams, and wares. After fried seafood at Cobie's Clam Shack, grab coffee at Snowy Owl Coffee Roasters to keep you warm as you walk along and marvel at the Brewster sand flats.

Chatham is a quintessential picturesque New England town perfect for strolling and browsing. It offers many boutique shops, restaurants, galleries, historic architectural gems, and scenic beaches, not to mention the Chatham Light Station looking out over the Atlantic Ocean. Consider visiting the Marconi-RCA Wireless Museum and the AWSC Shark Center while you're in town. Chatham can be quite crowded in the summer, so consider visiting in the shoulder season if you'd like more elbow room.

Considered the "heart of Cape Cod," **Dennis** boasts charming shops, restaurants, art galleries, and live music. For arts and culture lovers, visit the Cape Cod Museum of Art and Cape Cinema, a tiny nonprofit art house cinema that has been open since the 1930s. Be sure to arrive hungry at Sesuit Harbor Cafe, often ranked as serving the best lobster roll and fried seafood on the Cape, where you can also take in scenic views of the boats coming in and out of the harbor.

Eastham is less a town than a stretch of road offering gas, convenience stores, shops, markets, and restaurants for all your needs while visiting the Outer Cape or en route to the Nauset Light or Salt Pond Visitor Center.

Falmouth is a charming coastal town with a Main Street lined with gift, home decor, and clothing boutiques, art galleries, restaurants, and cafes where you can rest to take in beautiful views of the harbor. In the summer, this town is lively with farmers markets, movie nights, and live music. Be sure to spend time outdoors visiting the Nobska Point Light, catching some sun and waves at Old Silver Beach, and pedaling the Shining Sea Bikeway.

Comprising three tiny villages, **Orleans** is a relaxed seaside settlement boasting small-town charm with an edge of quirky. Here you can find art galleries and artist cottages, a bookstore, a community theater, evening concerts during the summer, and seafood restaurants. Bird Watcher's General Store is a mecca for bird lovers and Hot Chocolate Sparrow an institution for coffee and candy. After you grab a lobster roll at The Knack, be sure to grab a beach read at Sea Howl Bookshop before heading to Skaket Beach.

Provincetown is a vibrant, welcoming, and inclusive town packed with people during the summer months. Feast on seafood and Portuguese-inspired dishes, catch a drag or comedy show, or shop at boutiques and galleries all along Commercial Street, the heart of P-town. A storied and popular destination for artists, writers, and the LGBTQ+ community, this town will welcome you with open arms no matter who you are.

Settled in 1637, **Sandwich** is one of the oldest towns in the country. It maintains its historic charm and heritage in its preserved buildings and in museums like the Sandwich Glass Museum and the Heritage Museum and Gardens. Take a stroll along the Cape Cod Canal or along the boardwalk through a salt marsh.

Wellfleet is known for its oyster beds (home to its namesake, the Wellfleet oyster), seafood shacks, and restaurants. A charming and creative town, Wellfleet features many boutiques and art galleries, a drive-in theater and a live performance theater, as well as picturesque beaches and ocean views. For sand and sun, visit Marconi, Newcomb Hollow, and White Crest beaches. For a peaceful stroll through woodlands, beaches, ponds, and salt marshes, visit the Mass Audubon Wellfleet Bay Wildlife Sanctuary. Start your day at PB Boulangerie Bistro for pastries and coffee, then visit seafood institutions Moby Dick's Restaurant or Mac's Shack for lunch and dinner.

One of the oldest towns on the Cape, **Yarmouth** comprises three villages, with Yarmouth Port maintaining its historic charm. Here you can visit house museums, like the Edward Gorey House and the Captain Bangs Hallet House Museum. Be sure to stroll down The Captains' Mile, a road with more than fifty sea captain homes on either side (some still lived in, some converted to bed-and-breakfasts), identified with the black and gold oval Schooner Plaque awarded by the local historical society. Grab some popovers at Jack's Outback, get small-batch foods and lunch at Lighthouse Keeper's Pantry, and sit down at Leonessa or Inaho for dinner.

Where to Camp

Nickerson State Park, where the locals camp. This 1,900-acre state park in the heart of Cape Cod in Brewster offers a spacious campground with more than four hundred sites and endless recreation options like fishing, hiking, biking, swimming, paddling, visiting a playground, and more.

Shawme-Crowell State Forest, another beloved state park. This 700-acre pitch pine and scrub oak forest boasts a campground with many basic amenities you expect but is also uniquely and conveniently located near must-see cultural attractions like the Heritage Museum and Gardens and the Sandwich Glass Museum.

AutoCamp Cape Cod, if glamping is more your style. Check out this resort in Falmouth for a luxurious stay in beachside Airstreams—featuring amenities like à la carte meals from The Kitchen, and a general store with goods, snacks, and beverages.

Wellfleet Hollow State Campground, a quiet, quaint, no-frills campground in Wellfleet on the Cape Cod Rail Trail. Choose from a hundred or so sites and use this as a base camp to explore a creative and quirky town with excellent food options, picturesque ponds and marshes, and some of the best beaches on Cape Cod.

In addition to these public campgrounds, you can also arrange campsites through camping companies, such as Hipcamp, that provide access to private land and campsites while supporting local communities and preserving natural spaces.

Community Resources

Atlantic White Shark Conservancy (AWSC) is on a mission to support scientific research, improve public safety, and educate the community to inspire white shark conservation. The AWSC Shark Centers in Chatham and Provincetown are designed to engage the public in shark education through exhibits giving insight into white shark research, conservation, and natural history. The AWSC also offers shark excursions and private white shark charters to see these creatures in the wild.
atlanticwhiteshark.org

Barnstable Land Trust (BLT) is a nonprofit dedicated to preserving the natural resources and special places in and around Barnstable, Massachusetts. It serves as a leader in collaborative land conservation and stewardship, community engagement, and advocacy for the region's natural and cultural resources. BLT offers programs like Thoreau's Cape Cod Readathon, a two-day live reading of Henry David Thoreau's *Cape Cod* the organization staged to celebrate its fortieth anniversary year. It also spearheads a unique one-day regional tradition, First Day Hikes—free special walks, talks, and hikes led by more than fifteen conservation groups at multiple locations across Cape Cod on the first day of the new year, the only regional celebration of its kind in the nation.
blt.org

Cape and Islands Bookstore Trail is the result of Cape Cod book-sellers joining forces to create a trail celebrating the unique independent bookstores on Cape Cod, Martha's Vineyard, and Nantucket. The goal is to encourage visitors to explore towns across the Cape and recognize Cape Cod as a literary destination. A trail map can be downloaded from the website.
capeandislandsbookstoretrail.com

Cape Cod National Seashore was established in 1961 to protect the Outer Cape—a place of natural, historic, and cultural significance—from the development and commercialization happening elsewhere on Cape Cod. Much of the 40 miles and 44,000 acres of untamed sandy beaches, marshes, ponds, forests, lighthouses, wild cranberry bogs, walking trails, and dune shacks described in the stories in this book remain protected thanks to this designation. The national seashore has two visitor centers, the Salt Pond Visitor Center in Eastham and the Province Lands Visitor Center in Provincetown, both of which feature educational films, exhibits, souvenir shops, and information that is sure to enhance your appreciation and understanding of Cape Cod.
nps.gov/caco

Cape Cod Rail Trail is a paved, well-marked, and relatively flat bike trail that runs for more than 25 miles from South Dennis to South Wellfleet, passing through several towns, including Dennis, Harwich, Brewster, Orleans, and Eastham. Built on the right-of-way of an old railroad that transported freight and people for a hundred years, the trail is among the most scenic ways to experience Cape Cod.
mass.gov/locations/cape-cod-rail-trail

Center for Coastal Studies (CCS) is a nonprofit organization based in Provincetown that is dedicated to understanding, preserving, and protecting marine ecosystems and the coastal environment through applied research, education, and public policy initiatives. CCS collaborates with local, national, and international organizations and works with government agencies to promote environmental stewardship and develop policies and management strategies. It conducts research with emphasis on marine mammals of the western North Atlantic and on the coastal and marine habitats and resources of the Gulf of Maine; provides educational resources and programs encouraging the responsible use and conservation of coastal and marine ecosystems; and collaborates with other institutions and individuals to advance its mission.
coastalstudies.org

Dolphin Fleet's Whale Watch not only offers its passengers unforgettable memories out on the water with whales but also provides education and encourages understanding of the need to protect the whales, marine life, and habitats that are so important to those that live above and below the water. Dolphin Fleet participates in Whale SENSE, a program sponsored by NOAA and Whale and Dolphin Conservation that does educational outreach and recognizes whale-watching companies committed to responsible practices in the US Atlantic and Alaska.
whalewatch.com

Fine Arts Work Center (FAWC) in Provincetown is a culturally significant landmark where many of this collection's writers have practiced, taught, or exhibited. The center continues its legacy by providing artists and writers with studio facilities, live-work residences, a print shop, a reading library, a bookstore, and galleries where it hosts year-round readings, artist talks, exhibitions, and live performances.

fawc.org

Friends of the Cape Cod National Seashore (FCCNS) is a non-profit charitable organization operating under the jurisdiction of the National Park Service that has supported the national seashore since 1978 by raising funds for specific projects. Its efforts have maintained and restored trails and freshwater ponds, and provided funding for projects like the popular Cape Cod Symphony Orchestra summer concert series at the Salt Pond Visitor Center, the installation of exhibits along the Province Lands Bike Trail, the refurbishing of historic buildings like the Old Harbor Life-Saving Station, and educational events like the Science In the Seashore Symposium and the Winter Film Series at the Salt Pond Visitor Center.

fccns.org

International Fund for Animal Welfare (IFAW) is a global nonprofit helping animals and people thrive together. The IFAW plays an important role on Cape Cod by responding to distress calls and helping marine mammals affected by fishing gear entanglements, ocean noise, vessel collisions, and climate change. Its Marine Mammal Rescue program on Cape Cod has become a center of innovation and a symbol of hope for the global rescue community, revolutionizing how marine mammals are rescued, assessed, and released.

ifaw.org

Native Land Conservancy (NLC) is a native-led land conservancy protecting, sharing, and restoring land and water for the four-legged, the two-legged, the winged, and the finned. The organization focuses on land rescue—rescuing land through donation or title purchase, upholding conservation easements, and tending to its needs—as well as cultural preservation, providing space on these healthy landscapes for Indigenous people to safely practice their traditional cultural lifeways in their ancestral homelands.

nativelandconservancy.org

Woods Hole Oceanographic Institution (WHOI), located on the southwestern tip of Cape Cod, is an independent nonprofit organization dedicated exclusively to ocean research, technology, and education. It combines state-of-the-art science, engineering, and ship operations to unravel the mysteries of the deep and devise science-based solutions to planetwide problems.

whoi.edu

Essential Reads

The Outermost House: A Year of Life on the Great Beach of Cape Cod
by Henry Beston (originally published by Doubleday, 1928)

Colonization and the Wampanoag Story
by Linda Coombs (Crown Books for Young Readers, 2023)

Land's End: A Walk in Provincetown
by Michael Cunningham (Picador, 2012)

The Outer Beach: A Thousand-Mile Walk on Cape Cod's Atlantic Shore
by Robert Finch (W.W. Norton, 2018)

A Wild, Rank Place: One Year on Cape Cod
by David Gessner (University Press of New England, 1997)

From the Farther Shore: Discovering Cape Cod and the Islands Through Poetry
edited by Alice Kociemba, Robin Smith-Johnson, and Rich Youmans (Cultural Center of Cape Cod, 2021)

Later: My Life at the Edge of the World
by Paul Lisicky (Graywolf, 2020)

The Truro Bear and Other Adventures
by Mary Oliver (Beacon Press, 2008)

Six Walks: In the Footsteps of Henry David Thoreau
by Ben Shattuck (Tin House Books, 2022)

Cape Cod
by Henry David Thoreau (originally published by Ticknor and Fields, 1866)

Time and the Town: A Provincetown Chronicle
by Mary Heaton Vorse (originally published by Dial Press, 1942)

Acknowledgments

Working on this book series as parents to two young kids has required a village. Ilyssa, first and foremost, would like to thank Dave for supporting and encouraging her enthusiasm for this new *Campfire Stories* series and her decision to not plow right into a new job. With Ilyssa taking the lead on travel to research these books, Dave took on the primary responsibility for cooking every meal, doing every school or activity drop-off and pickup for two kids at two different schools, conducting the bedtime routine *every night*, and generally keeping our kids alive, full of snacks, and happy—often for a week at a time. Without Dave's unwavering belief in Ilyssa's passion and ideas, in addition to his editing and writing contributions, there would be no *Campfire Stories*. We'd also like to thank Ilyssa's mom, Diane Shapiro, who supports us during these times of travel and writing—and our many friends who host the girls for playdates and sleepovers.

Our daughters, Lula and Isla, also deserve thanks for inspiring us to pursue our passions and for their patience and understanding when we have to travel—even when it makes them feel like *a barnacle drifting all alone at sea*.

We are so grateful to Kate Rogers, editor in chief of Mountaineers Books, who curiously continues to entertain our *many* ideas, and—with honesty and great wisdom—helps to refine and shepherd them into the world. We extend this appreciation to the rest of the Mountaineers Books team, whose enthusiasm for our projects is deeply felt—and with a special shout-out to Joleen Simmons, who makes us feel like rock stars. To our editing team, Beth Jusino and Lorraine Anderson—we are grateful for your meticulous editorial work, and we admire your ability to take on a massive collection of stories spanning many centuries with enthusiasm and patience.

This series would not be what it is without Melissa McFeeters, who has been with us from the very beginning and has designed all of our *Campfire Stories* projects—likely the reason you, reader, picked up our book in the first place!

We'd also like to thank the writers, librarians, researchers, and staff and/or volunteers at the many nonprofit organizations and museums we've connected with across Cape Cod for your generosity and time. Our understanding of these places without your personal stories, lived experiences and history, and special connections to them would be far less authentic, passionate, and informed. We'd especially like to thank Liz Bradfield, who not only generously shared her time with us walking across and along the beaches of Truro, but also gave us one of the most memorable experiences, inviting us along on a chartered boat to watch whales off the cape's coast. We'd also like to thank Sue Sullivan and Janet Milkman of Barnstable Land Trust for sharing your love of the Cape; Gabrielle Faria-Kalkanis at the Sturgis Library for giving us a head start in our literary journey of the cape; Marianne Walsh of the Atlantic White Shark Conservancy for reminding us why sharks ought to be seen more as friends than enemies; and Catherine Rogers for sharing her knowledge of the Cape to strengthen our recommendations.

To the bookstore buyers and staff who take time to chat with us while we're on our research trips, who educate us on local writers and important literature as well as carve a little space on your shelves for our book or feature it in your beautiful, creative displays—we see you and we appreciate you. We can't express how delighted we are to receive texts from friends and family traveling across the US who spot our books or card decks in the wild, or when we ourselves encounter them in real life. It never gets old.

Last, to our dear readers, whose insatiable desire for stories from our wild places allows us to continue collecting stories—we are grateful for your curiosity, love for our natural world, and desire to follow in the age-old tradition of storytelling. Without those readers who reached out or attended our events to say, *When are you going to do MY favorite place in the world?* or challenged us to consider places outside of national parks, we wouldn't have this new series.

Permissions
and Sources

Davis, Jarita. "Harvesting a Return." Printed with the permission of the author.

Doty, Mark. "Long Point Light" © 1994. Printed with the permission of the author.

Gessner, David. "Following Thoreau" from *A Wild, Rank Place* by David Gessner (Brandeis University Press). Copyright © 2012 by David Gessner. Used by permission.

Koscher, Adeline Carrie. "Learning to Live with Water." Printed with the permission of the author.

Kunitz, Stanley. "The Wellfleet Whale". Copyright © 1985 by Stanley Kunitz, from THE COLLECTED POEMS by Stanley Kunitz. Used by permission of W. W. Norton & Company, Inc.

Leighton, Clare. "The Beach" from *Where Land Meets Sea: The Tide Line of Cape Cod* by Clare Leighton. Copyright 1954, © 1973 by Clare Leighton. Reprinted with the permission of The Permissions Company, LLC, on behalf of David R. Godine, Publisher, Inc., godine.com.

Oliver, Mary. From American Primitive by Mary Oliver, copyright ©1983. Reprinted by permission of Little, Brown, an imprint of Hachette Book Group, Inc.

Petiet, Mary. "Rock." Printed with the permission of the author.

Vorse, Mary Heaton. Excerpts from *Time and the Town: A Provincetown Chronicle*, edited by Adele Heller with cooperation of Jill O'Brien. New Brunswick, NJ: Rutgers University Press, 1991. Copyright © 1942 by Mary Heaton Vorse. Reprinted by permission of Rutgers University Press.

SOURCES

Civilian New York City. "A Writer's Retreat: Michael Cunningham on Provincetown." *Civilian,* 7 May 2013, civilianglobal.com/features/michael-cunningham-on-provincetown/.

Duenwald, Mary. "The Land and Words of Mary Oliver, the Bard of Provincetown." *New York Times*, 1 July 2009, www.nytimes.com/2009/07/05/travel/05oliver.html.

"Dune Shacks." Provincetown Community Compact, thecompact.org/dune-shacks.html.

Evans, Tony Tekaroniake. "Who Was Squanto, and What Was His Role in the First Thanksgiving?" History, A&E Television Networks, 21 November 2022, www.history.com/news /squanto-pilgrims-help-plymouth-thanksgiving.

Greenfield, Beth. "Trading One Beach Retreat for Another." *New York Times*, 8 June 2007, www.nytimes.com/2007/06/08 /realestate/greathomes/08away.html.

Harrison, Sue. "Mary Heaton Vorse Is Coming Home." *Provincetown Independent*, 24 August 2022, provincetownindependent .org/arts-minds/2022/08/24/mary-heaton-vorse-is-coming-home/.

"The Industrious Artist: Clare Leighton." *Pallant House Magazine*, October 2013, pallant.org.uk/the-industrious-artist-clare -leighton/.

Laborde, Monique. "Provincetown Remembers Mary Oliver." GBH, 28 January 2019, www.wgbh.org/news/local/2019-01-28 /provincetown-remembers-mary-oliver.

Lelli, Barbara, David E. Harris, and AbouEl-Makarim Aboueissa. "Seal Bounties in Maine and Massachusetts, 1888 to 1962," *Northeastern Naturalist*, 1 July 2009, doi.org/10.1656 /045.016.0206.

"Marine Mammal Rescue Meets Conservation." IFAW, www.ifaw.org/projects/saving-whales-dolphins-porpoises.

"Mark Doty." Poetry Foundation, www.poetryfoundation.org /poets/mark-doty.

"Native Land." Native Land Digital, native-land.ca.

Nunes, Alex, and Ana González. "The Big Immigration Story Behind a Small Berry." The Public's Radio, *Mosaic* podcast,

episode 28/season 1, 2 January 2020, explore.thepublicsradio
.org/stories/the-big-immigration-story-behind-a-small-berry/

Russell, Jenna. "The Fight Over the Dune Shacks of Cape Cod:
No Power, No Water—but Eugene O'Neill Was Here." *New
York Times*, 6 August 2023, www.nytimes.com/2023/08/06/us
/cape-cod-dune-shacks.html.

Silverman, David J. "In 1621, the Wampanoag Tribe Had Its Own
Agenda." *Atlantic*, 27 November 2019, www.theatlantic.com/
ideas/archive/2019/11/thanksgiving-belongs-wampanoag
-tribe/602422/.

"Stellwagen Bank National Marine Sanctuary." stellwagen.noaa
.gov/.

"Vessel Impacts: Stellwagen Bank." sanctuaries.noaa.gov/science
/sentinel-site-program/stellwagen-bank/vessel-impacts.html.

"Wampanoag History." Wampanoag Tribe of Gay Head (Aquinnah), wampanoagtribe-nsn.gov/wampanoag-history#.

Directory

FALMOUTH
falmouthvisitor.com

Añejo Mexican Bistro
anejo.cc
188 Main St

AutoCamp Cape Cod
autocamp.com/cape-cod
836 Palmer Ave

Bad Martha Farmer's Brewery
*badmarthabeer.com/falmouth
-brewery*
876 E Falmouth Hwy,
East Falmouth

Betsy's Diner
betsys-diner.business.site
457 Main St

Flying Bridge Restaurant
flyingbridgerestaurant.com
220 Scranton Ave

Nobska Light
friendsofnobska.org
233 Nobska Rd

Old Silver Beach
296 Quaker Rd

Quarterdeck Restaurant
qdfalmouth.com
164 Main St

**Smitty's Homemade
Ice Cream**
facebook.com/smittysic
326 E Falmouth Hwy,
East Falmouth

Statue of Rachel Carson
Waterfront Park,
112–138 Water St

MASHPEE
*mashpeewampanoagtribe
-nsn.gov*

Mashpee Commons
mashpeecommons.com
22 Steeple St

**Mashpee Wampanoag
Tribe Museum**
*mashpeewampanoagtribe-nsn
.gov/museum*
414 Main St

Naukabout Brewing
naukabout.com
13 Lake Ave

SANDWICH
sandwichmass.org
....

**Cape Cod
Cranberry Bog Tours**
capecodcranberrybogtours.com
30 Roos Rd, East Sandwich

**Dunbar House Tea Room
and Wine Bar**
thedunbarhouse.com
1 Water St

**Fishermen's View Seafood
Market and Restaurant**
fishermensview.com
20 Freezer Rd

**Heritage Museums
& Gardens**
heritagemuseumsandgardens.org
67 Grove St

Sandwich Boardwalk
103 Wood Ave

Sandwich Glass Museum
sandwichglassmuseum.org
129 Main St

Shawme-Crowell State Forest
*mass.gov/locations/shawme
-crowell-state-forest*
42 Main St

The Brown Jug
thebrownjug.com
155 Main St

**Thornton W. Burgess Society
Nature Center and Jam
Kitchen**
thorntonburgess.org
6 Discovery Hill Rd,
East Sandwich

Titcomb's Bookshop
titcombsbookshop.com
432 Route 6A, East Sandwich

WOODS HOLE
woodshole.com
....

Masterson Made
mastersonmade.com
98 Water St

**Ocean Science
Discovery Center**
*whoi.edu/who-we-are/visit-whoi
/ocean-science-exhibit-center*
15 School Street

**Pie in the Sky
Bakery and Cafe**
piecoffee.com
10 Water St

Woods Hole Oceanographic Institution Visitor Center and Store
whoi.edu/who-we-are/visit-whoi /visitor-center
93 Water Street

Woods Hole Science Aquarium
fisheries.noaa.gov/about/woods -hole-science-aquarium
166 Water St

MID CAPE

BARNSTABLE
town.barnstable.ma.us

Barnstable Market
barnstablemarket.com
3220 Main St

Hyannis Whale Watcher Cruises
whales.net
269 Millway

Mass Audubon Long Pasture Wildlife Sanctuary
massaudubon.org/longpasture
345 Bone Hill Rd

Mattakeese Wharf Seafood
mattakeese.com
273 Millway

Nirvana Coffee Company
nirvanacoffeecompany.com
3206 Main St

Sturgis Library
sturgislibrary.org
3090 Main St

DENNIS
visitdennis.com

Annie's Crannies
anniescrannies.com
36 Scarsdale Rd

Cape Cinema
capecinema.org
35 Hope Ln

Cape Cod Museum of Art
ccmoa.org
60 Hope Ln

Dennis Village Mercantile
dennisvillagemercantile.com
778 Main St

Encore Bistro and Bar
encorediningcapecod.com
36 Hope Ln

Harvest Bar and Gallery
harvestgallery.co
776 Main St

Sesuit Harbor Cafe
sesuit-harbor-cafe.com
357 Sesuit Neck Rd

YARMOUTH PORT
yarmouth.ma.us

Edward Gorey House
edwardgoreyhouse
8 Strawberry Ln

Inaho Sushi
inaho-sushi.com
157 Main St

Jack's Outback II
Jacksoutback2.com
161 Main St

Leonessa
leonessacapecod.com
43 Main St

**Lighthouse Keeper's
Cafe and Pantry**
lighthousekeeperspantry.com
173 Main St

LOWER CAPE

BREWSTER
brewster-ma.gov

Brewster Book Store
brewsterbookstore.com
2648 Main St

Brewster Fish House
brewsterfishhousecapecod.com
2208 Main St

Brewster Flats
brewster-ma.gov
Access from any public beach
in Brewster

Cafe Alfresco
cafealfrescocapecod.com
1097 Main St

**Cape Cod Museum
of Natural History**
ccmnh.org
869 Main St

Cobies Clam Shack
cobies.com
3260 Main St

Nickerson State Park
*mass.gov/locations/
nickerson-state-park*
3488 Main St

Snowy Owl Coffee Roasters
socoffee.co
2624 Main St

The Brewster Store
brewsterstore.com
1935 Main St

CHATHAM
chatham-ma.gov

AWSC Shark Center
*atlanticwhiteshark.org/
shark-center-chatham*
235 Orleans Rd

Chatham Bars Inn
chathambarsinn.com
297 Shore Rd

Chatham Light Station
*historic-chatham.org
/lighthouse.html*
37 Main St

Del Mar Bar and Bistro
delmarbistro.com
907 Main St

Impudent Oyster
theimpudentoyster.com
15 Chatham Bars Ave

Kream N' Kone
kreamnkonechatham.com
1653 Main St

**Mac's Chatham
Fish and Lobster**
chathamfish.com
1291 Main St

**Marconi-RCA
Wireless Museum**
chathammarconi.org
847 Orleans Rd

Mom and Pops Burgers
momandpopschatham.com
1603 Main St

**Monomoy National
Wildlife Refuge**
fws.gov/refuge/monomoy
30 Wikis Way

HARWICH
harwich-ma.gov

Brax Landing Restaurant
braxrestaurant.com
705 Route 28

Cranberry Bog Tours
cranberrybogtours.com
1601 Factory Rd

Cranberry Harvest
cranberryharvest.com
33 Rocky Way

Old Colony Rail Trail
*traillink.com/trail/
old-colony-rail-trail*
Harwich to Chatham

ORLEANS
town.orleans.ma.us

Bird Watcher's General Store
birdwatchersgeneralstore.com
36 Route 6A

Hot Chocolate Sparrow
hotchocolatesparrow.com
5 Old Colony Way

Land-Ho!
land-ho.com
38 Main Street

Sea Howl Bookshop
seahowlbookshop.com
46 Main St

Skaket Beach
192 Skaket Beach Rd

The Knack
theknackcapecod.com
5 Route 6A

OUTER CAPE

EASTHAM
eastham-ma.gov

Hole in One Bakery and Coffee Shop
theholecapecod.com
4295 Route 6

Mac's Market and Kitchen Eastham
*macsseafood.com/restaurant/
macs-market-kitchen-eastham*
4680 Route 6

Nauset Light
nausetlight.org
120 Nauset Light Beach Rd

Salt Pond Visitor Center
nps.gov/caco
50 Nauset Rd

PROVINCETOWN
ptowntourism.com

Blackwater Pond
Access via Beech Forest Trail,
36 Race Point Rd
*nps.gov/caco/planyourvisit/
beechforest.htm*

Dune Shack Trail
Route 6 at Snail Road

East End Books Ptown
eastendbooksptown.com
389 Commercial St

Jimmy's Hideaway
jimmyshideaway.com
179 Commercial St

Liz's Cafe, Anybody's Bar
lizscafeptown.com
31 Bradford St

Long Point Light Station
*lighthousefoundation.org/
lighthouses/long-point-light*
Cape Cod National Seashore

Mac's Fish House
*macsseafood.com/restaurant/
macs-fish-house-provincetown*
85 Shank Painter Rd

**Old Harbor
Life-Saving Station**
*nps.gov/caco/learn
/historyculture/old-harbor
-life-saving-station.htm*
Race Point Beach

**Peaked Hill Bars
Historic District**
*nps.gov/caco/learn/history
culture/dune-shacks-of-peaked
-hill-bars-historic-district.htm*
Cape Cod National Seashore

**Pilgrim Monument and
Provincetown Museum**
pilgrim-monument.org
1 High Pole Hill Rd

**Province Lands
Visitor Center**
nps.gov/caco
171 Race Point Rd

**Provincetown
Portuguese Bakery**
*provincetownportuguesebakery
.com*
299 Commercial St

Provincetown Public Library
provincetownlibrary.org
356 Commercial St

Race Point Beach
*nps.gov/caco/planyourvisit
/race-point-beach.htm*
Cape Cod National Seashore

Race Point Light Station
racepointlighthouse.org
Cape Cod National Seashore

Spiritus Pizza
spirituspizza.com
190 Commercial St

Tim's Used Books
242 Commercial St

**Wood End Light
Lookout Station**
*lighthousefoundation.org
/lighthouses/wood-end-light*
Cape Cod National Seashore

TRURO
truro-ma.gov

Head of the Meadow Beach
*nps.gov/caco/planyourvisit
/head-of-the-meadow.htm*
Cape Cod National Seashore

Highland Light
highlandlighthouse.org
27 Highland Light Rd, North
Truro

Pamet Cranberry Bog Trail
*nps.gov/caco/planyourvisit
/pamet-area-trails.htm*
111 N Pamet Rd

Salty Market
thesaltymarket.com
2 Highland Rd, North Truro

WELLFLEET
wellfleet-ma.gov

Mac's Shack
*macsseafood.com/restaurant
/macs-shack-wellfleet*
91 Commercial St

Mass Audubon Wellfleet Bay Wildlife Sanctuary
massaudubon.org/wellfleetbay
291 Route 6, South Wellfleet

Moby Dick's Restaurant
mobys.com
3225 Route 6

PB Boulangerie Bistro
pbboulangeriebistro.com
15 LeCount Hollow Rd, South Wellfleet

The Wicked Oyster
thewickedo.com
50 Main St

Wellfleet Drive-In Theatre
wellfleetcinemas.com/drive-in-theatre
51 Route 6

Wellfleet Hollow State Campground
mass.gov/locations/wellfleet-hollow-state-campground
180 Old Kings Hwy

About the Contributors

Mary Bergman is a writer whose work is dedicated to documenting and preserving the unique ways of life of people living by the sea. She can be heard as a contributor to *A Cape Cod Notebook*, a weekly nature/natural world radio essay program on WCAI, the Cape and Islands NPR station, and her work has also appeared in *Historic Nantucket, N Magazine, The Common online, McSweeney's Internet Tendency, Provincetown Arts,* and other places where great stories are told.

Henry Beston (1888–1968) was an American writer and naturalist best known for his work *The Outermost House*, published in 1928 and considered a classic of nature writing. Beston had served as an ambulance driver with the French army in World War I and after the war retreated to a 16-by-20-foot house on the beach at Eastham in search of peace and solitude. He stayed there on and off for about two years, and the book he wrote about his experience has been credited as one of the motivating factors behind the designation of the Cape Cod National Seashore.

Elizabeth Bradfield is the author of five poetry collections, most recently *Toward Antarctica*, and co-editor of the anthologies *Cascadia Field Guide: Art, Ecology, Poetry* and *Broadsided Press: Fifteen*

ABOUT THE CONTRIBUTORS   185

Years of Poetic/Artistic Collaboration. Editor-in-chief of Broadsided, Liz lives on Cape Cod, works as a marine naturalist, and teaches at Brandeis University.

Linda Coombs is an author and historian from the Wampanoag Tribe of Gay Head, and the former program director of the Aquinnah Cultural Center. Wampanoag leaders are actively working to reclaim their story, and Linda's book *Colonization and the Wampanoag Story* pictures the tribe before colonization, living in harmony with the abundance of the Cape Cod seashore.

Michael Cunningham is a novelist, screenwriter, and producer who splits his time between New York City and Provincetown. His 1998 novel *The Hours* won the Pulitzer Prize for Fiction and the PEN/Faulkner Award in 1999. Cunningham has taught at the Fine Arts Work Center in Provincetown and is a lecturer in creative writing at Yale.

Cass Daubenspeck is a writing and literature teacher in Pennsylvania, and has lived in and written about the varied landscapes of California's Central Valley, New York City's outer boroughs, and the wilderness of New England. Growing up in the Nauset Lighthouse on Cape Cod, she has always been interested in the cultural and historical significance of the Outer Cape region and how historical sites like Nauset Light can contribute to the public's understanding and appreciation of the area's natural surroundings.

Jarita Davis is a poet and fiction writer who lives in West Falmouth and works for NOAA Fisheries in Woods Hole. She was the writer in residence at the Nantucket Historical Association and has received fellowships from the Mellon Mayes program, Cave Canem, Hedgebrook, and the Disquiet International Literary Program in Lisbon. Her work has appeared in *Southwestern Review, Historic Nantucket,*

Cave Canem Anthologies, Crab Orchard Review, Plainsongs, Verdad Magazine, and *Cape Cod Poetry Review*. Her first poetry collection, *Return Flights,* was published by Tagus Press in March 2016.

Mark Doty is an American poet and memoirist, best known for his book *My Alexandria*, a collection of poetry centered around the themes of mortality and life, beauty and loss, during the AIDS/HIV crisis, which was selected for the National Poetry Series and earned him the National Book Critics Circle Award, the Los Angeles Times Book Prize, and the T. S. Eliot Prize, Britain's most significant annual award for poetry. His memoirs include the award-winning *New York Times* best seller *Dog Years*. He is currently a distinguished professor and writer-in-residence in the Department of English at Rutgers University.

David Gessner is the author of thirteen books that blend a love of nature, humor, memoir, and environmentalism, including *All the Wild That Remains, Return of the Osprey, Sick of Nature,* and *Leave It as It Is: A Journey Through Theodore Roosevelt's American Wilderness*. His awards include a Pushcart Prize and the John Burroughs Award. He is a professor of creative writing at the University of North Carolina, Wilmington, and founder of the literary magazine *Ecotone*.

Adeline Carrie Koscher lives and writes on Cape Cod. She crafts strange, little works of fiction and poetry as a conduit for wonder, solace, and vitality. Koscher's chapbook of poetry, *Liquid Song,* was published in April 2020 by Finishing Line Press. Her writing can be found in *Review Americana, The Lyon Review, Adana, Altered States, ninepatch, Zetetic, Claudius Speaks, Novelty,* and *Canary*.

Stanley Kunitz (1905–2006) became the country's tenth poet laureate, the highest literary honor in America, at the age of ninety-five, when he was still actively writing, publishing, and promoting poetry. He taught at a variety of universities (including a long stint at Columbia University) and greatly influenced succeeding generations of poets. He was awarded the Pulitzer Prize in poetry for his third collection, *Selected Poems: 1928–1958*, published in 1959. Among many other honors were a National Book Award and a National Medal of Arts.

Artist and writer **Clare Leighton** (1898–1989) was best known for her wood engravings and prints that largely depicted pastoral life and various laborers. She created nearly nine hundred woodblocks in her lifetime, which were exhibited around the world and published in more than twelve of her own books. Her writings include the 1954 book *Where Land Meets Sea*, about her experiences on Cape Cod.

Mary Oliver (1935–2019) was born in Ohio but adopted New England as her home, moving to Provincetown in the 1960s to live with her long-time love, Molly Malone Cook. There she found inspiration for the nature poetry that made her the country's best-selling poet. She became one of the first faculty members at the Fine Arts Work Center in Provincetown and established the writing fellowship program there. She won the Pulitzer Prize for *American Primitive* in 1984 and the American Book Award for *New and Selected Poems* in 1992.

Mary Petiet is an author, poet, and publisher whose writing is deeply influenced by Cape Cod's nature and inspirational energy. Her work emphasizes our connection to each other and the natural world, focusing on positive empowerment. In 2020 she founded Sea Crow Press, an independent publishing company dedicated to amplifying the voices of humans, animals, and the land.

Henry David Thoreau (1817–1862) made his name with his 1854 book *Walden*, an account of twenty-six months (1845–1847) spent living simply in a one-room cabin on the shores of Walden Pond in Massachusetts. While writing that book, the naturalist, essayist, poet, and philosopher took a few trips to Cape Cod and documented his observations of the natural world there in a book published in 1865. Thoreau is also remembered for his essay "Civil Disobedience," inspired by the night he spent in jail for refusing to pay poll taxes because of his opposition to the Mexican-American War and slavery.

Activist, pioneering journalist, and author **Mary Heaton Vorse** (1874–1966) was a prominent figure in social justice movements and in journalism, reporting on world wars, labor disputes, and the experience of immigrants, and protesting for women's suffrage. In her autobiography, she described herself as "a woman who in early life got angry because many children lived miserably and died needlessly." She lived in Provincetown every summer of her life from 1906 until her death in 1966 and highlighted her connection to the region in her essay collection *Time and the Town*.

About the Editors

Ilyssa Kyu is the founder of Amble, a sabbatical program for creative professionals to take time away with purpose in support of nature conservancies. She is a design researcher and strategist with a degree in industrial design and previously worked at boutique and global design studios. She is currently using her design consulting experience to support nature nonprofits through All Hands, a creative collective, as well as continually dreaming up ways to integrate her love for storytelling and the outdoors.

Dave Kyu is a socially engaged artist and writer. Born in Seoul, South Korea, and raised in the United States, he explores the creative tensions of identity, community, and public space in his work. He has managed public arts projects for the Asian Arts Initiative, Mural Arts, and the City of Philadelphia. His own creative projects have found him commissioning skywriting planes to write messages 10,000 feet above Philadelphia and doing everything Facebook told him to do for a month.

Together, they've created the *Campfire Stories* book and card deck series. They were artists-in-residence at Independence National Historical Park in Philadelphia, PA—a collaboration between the NEA, the National Park Service, and the Mural Arts Program—which resulted in an event, "I Will Hold You in the Light," which brought together six diverse performers responding to the theme of "The Pursuit of Happiness."

recreation • lifestyle • conservation

MOUNTAINEERS BOOKS, including its two imprints, Skipstone and Braided River, is a leading publisher of quality outdoor recreation, sustainability, and conservation titles. As a 501(c)(3) nonprofit, we are committed to supporting the environmental and educational goals of our organization by providing expert information on human-powered adventure, sustainable practices at home and on the trail, and preservation of wilderness.

Our publications are made possible through the generosity of donors, and through sales of 700 titles on outdoor recreation, sustainable lifestyle, and conservation. To donate, purchase books, or learn more, visit us online:

MOUNTAINEERS BOOKS
1001 SW Klickitat Way, Suite 201 • Seattle, WA 98134
800-553-4453 • mbooks@mountaineersbooks.org
www.mountaineersbooks.org

An independent nonprofit publisher since 1960

YOU MAY ALSO LIKE: